THE
TRADING METHODS
OF W.D. GANN

The
Trading Methods
of W.D. Gann

HOW TO BUILD YOUR TECHNICAL ANALYSIS TOOLBOX

Hima Reddy

HimaReddy.com

Contents

Second Editon, 2020

In memory of my father, Pandu R. Tadoori,
who ignited my passion for the markets and
led the way to my own financial freedom.

Praise for The Trading Methods of W.D. Gann

"The book is written for those that want to make money in the markets. I **am an intraday futures trader and find the trading methodologies very useful. You could make a lifetime of studying Gann; the book lays out the important works.** Trading is about understanding the charts and what they are telling us, where the entry and exit is. This book covers the Gann material and how to apply it." – Andrew H., New York

"Perfect for the beginner wanting to learn about technical analysis from a grass roots level. **Lots of simple and easy to understand diagrams, well-described and not buried in acronyms.** Once you have read this, you can start reading Ganns' actual works and understand the meanings behind the concepts that he writes about. His work assumes you already have a lot of stock market background, so you get lost in the terminology and unique language of the stock market without a good foundation." – Alan L.

"I have hunted to get education to get my Gann Trading skills up to start. I needed this to clarify the base parts of the theory. Using a lot of techniques in this book, **I have had a very good 3 non-losing, successful trading weeks!** A great THANK YOU to the author!" - Daniel C.

"Beyond being a concise introduction to Gann, this book is a wonderful primer on trade discipline and money management for this reason alone **this book will pay dividends for serious students of technical analysis, trading and money management.**" – Joshua R.

"This book was very good. I "never" thought I'd understand Gann, as everything I'd heard seemed unintelligible, and as a consequence I didn't like Gann, but **Hima Reddy did all the work and made Gann's trading rules eminently understandable, with rules translated into concepts described in the text and fully annotated on the charts. Now I can say I like Gann.** I only hope Hima will go into advanced Gann topics, to get into the meaning and use of Gann's esoteric mathematical methods if useful, or applicable as tools." - S. James

"I admire the author for explaining Gann's principles which were so central to her career. **It is interesting to compare Gann's way of explaining technical analysis and technical trading to the "modern" concepts and terminology used today.**

Unlike many books on trading, this one **clearly explains a variety of entry and exit signals for trading which are applicable to any underlying instruments in any time frame.** I applaud Ms. Reddy's excellent work." H. Camper

"Hima Reddy takes the ideas of W.D. Gann and simplifies them so they are understandable. **This book is chock full of examples of the technical analysis of W.D. Gann and how they are applied. Graphics are excellent here.** Add this to your library of quantitative analysis textbooks." Wizard D.

"Readers are provided with **easy to understand and digest tidbits** on Gann's Principles and Rules **with clear examples**." - Tristan A.

"**This book was easy to read even with little trading experience.** She includes a lot of charts which allow the reader to follow his thought processes and even analyze them for themselves. **This book is a must-read for those looking to acquire some basic knowledge of technical analysis.**" - M. Bey

Introduction

"Life affords no greater pleasure than that of helping others who are trying to help themselves." – W.D. Gann

When I was 16 years old, I was doing chemistry homework one night and stopped in my father's office to get some assistance with my assignment. I saw my father studying a graph of some sort displayed on his computer screen. I asked him what he was looking at and he said it was a chart of a stock, plotting the changes in its price, and he said he was using the chart to help him trade the stock.

When I asked how he was doing that, he explained that he was using the mathematical relationships present in the stock's price history to help him determine whether the price of the stock would likely go up or down, so that he could buy or sell shares of the stock accordingly.

I was intrigued—I've always been a "math geek", so it wasn't surprising—and I told my father that I wanted to know more about this type of financial analysis. I asked him about the possibilities of learning more about it in college, and he told me that it was not very popular and that I likely would not come across it while at school. However, he did offer to help me learn about trading through books and following his stock charts.

Over the next few months, he gave me his old edition (printed in 1976) of Gann's *How to Make Profits Trading in Commodities*. He told me to read that book over and over and glean Gann's methods from it. Seventeen years later, he still gave me the same advice—to keep studying the works of Gann's great mind and incorporate what I learn into my own trading plan.

Back when I was in high school and college, as a young person with no experience with the markets, I had to teach myself the methods that were presented in Gann's works. I did this by synthesizing the concepts into smaller pieces that I could grasp.

With knowledge gained through these smaller tenets, I annotated charts—a countless number and variety—on my computer as well as by hand. I then synthesized the buy and sell signals and trade management concepts that I understood and witnessed into my own trading plan, for which I continued to collect examples of charts that illustrated the relating theories.

I even began to create market newsletters for myself, focusing in on one security at a time and looking at its key price points. This was all to help me better understand Gann's main points and methods so that I could profitably apply them to my trading.

I eventually obtained my Chartered Market Technician (CMT), a designation administered by The CMT Association. I then worked as a professional technical analyst for several years; however, what I learned from Gann's teachings has remained my prime trading guide.

The chapters ahead contain my humble attempt to re-present my self-taught interpretation of some of Gann's major works. His writings are among the most esoterically written technical analysis materials out there. However, over the course of my study I have been able to make them "my own."

Anyone who has looked at Gann's works sees that he used many chart examples to illustrate his trading rules and philosophies. I will do the same, and I will expand the realm to include securities that many of us observe regularly. I will apply the trading rules and ideas to modern charts, making them accessible to the modern trader.

In 2016 my father passed away suddenly, leaving a big hole in our lives. He is the reason that I am sharing this with you today. His foresight secured my financial future and I want to pass on his legacy to as many traders as I can reach. That is my 'Why' and the bigger reason I began teaching Gann's little-understood methods.

I hope you, the reader, find that this will help you to improve your own "trading toolkit". My goal is not to make you a "Gann expert" through this book alone—I believe trading education is an ongoing process and can't come from any one person or resource. I do, however, hope that I am speaking to the part of you that is akin to the sixteen-year old I once was—eager to venture into deeper study of Gann's materials for the most complete approach to this master's investing methodologies.

In order to keep the explanations with their chart or illustrations, you will find some extra white space or 'gaps' in the text on the page. Gaps in the market are often filled! Feel free to fill this "gap" with YOUR notes as you move through the book :)

I love working with and rewarding Action Takers. Money loves Speed and Action! So I am gifting you a companion guide that pulls out the following charts and expands them into full 8.5 x 11 size, so you can print out the charts larger and in full color.

Download and Print your Companion Guide FIRST, before you dive into the teaching, at himareddy.com/gann2bonus

1

The Work of W.D. Gann

Market Predictions

As an author, I want to give you a reason to read this book that goes beyond my promise that the material is useful. So, I would like to refer you to some of Gann's greatest market predictions and how he profited from those moves.

Throughout Gann's works, he advised his students to use all of their forecasting and trading tools all of the time to discover the forces at work in any given market. Therefore, sharing his forecasting/trading successes should give you confidence that the information ahead in this book will help improve **your own** investing methods.

One of the most concise and publicly accessible records of Gann's market predictions is an article written by Richard D. Wyckoff in December 1909. The title of the article is '*William D. Gann: An Operator Whose Science and Ability Place Him in the Front Rank—His Remarkable Predictions and Trading Record*'.

The article was published in Volume 5 (Number 2) of the *Ticker and Investment Digest*, a very influential stock market publication at the time.

The first part of the article is a direct exploration of Gann's general methods of market analysis. Later in the article, Wyckoff shares the findings of William E. Gilley, who was brought in to validate the success (or failure) of Gann's methods.

Gilley was an Inspector of Imports in New York with twenty-five years experience with the markets. During the time that Gilley observed Gann, he watched Gann make 286 trades. 264 of those were winning trades, equaling a success rate of 92 percent![1]

Above all, Gilley documented a series of predictions that Gann made during October 1909. Some of Gann's more remarkable predictions were as follows:

Union Pacific (stock)

"In 1908 when Union Pacific was 168 ⅛, he told me that it would not touch 169 before it had a good break. We sold it short all the way down to 152 ⅜, covering on the weak spots and putting it out again on the rallies, securing a 23 points profit out of an eighteen-point move."

United States Steel (stock)

"He came to me when United States Steel was selling around 50 and said 'This Steel will run up from 58 but it will not sell at 59. From there it should break 16 ¾ points.' We sold it short around 58 ⅜ with a stop at 59. The highest it went was 58 ¾. From there it declined to 41 ¼ - 17 ½ points."

United States Steel

"In our presence Mr. Gann sold Steel common short at 94 ⅞, saying that it would not go to 95. It did not.

On a drive which occurred during the week ending October 29th, Mr. Gann bought Steel common at 86 ¼, saying that it would not go to 86. The lowest it sold was 86 ⅛."

Wheat (commodity futures)

"At another time wheat was selling at about 89c. He predicted that the May option would sell at $1.35. We bought it and made large profits on the way up. It actually touched $1.35 ½."

Wheat

"One of the most astonishing calculations made by Mr. Gann was during last summer (1909) when he predicted that September wheat would sell at $1.20. This meant that it must touch that figure before the end of the month of September.

At twelve o'clock, Chicago time, on September 30th (the last day) the option was selling below $1.08, and it looked as though his prediction would not be fulfilled. Mr. Gann said 'If it does not touch $1.20 by the close of the market it will prove that there is something wrong with my whole method of calculation. I do not care what price it is now, it must go there.'

It is common history that September wheat surprised the whole country by selling at $1.20 and no higher in the very last hour of the trading, closing at that figure."

I hope that Gilley's observations presented within the context of Wyckoff's article have brought your attention to what Gann was able to accomplish investing in the markets. Gann dedicated his life's work to understanding the markets and the principles which govern them, and it is no small feat to have such insight into the markets. This is why what Gann had to share is of such great value. The lessons taught in those pages are among the tools that he used to master the market as he did.

Publications

- *Truth of the Stock Tape* (1923)
- *Tunnel Thru The Air* (1927)
- *Wall Street Stock Selector* (1930)
- *New Stock Trend Detector* (1936)
- *How to Make Profits Trading in Puts and Calls* (1937)
- *Face Facts America* (1940)
- *How to Make Profits Trading in Commodities* (1941)
- *45 Years in Wall Street* (1949)
- *Magic Word* (1950)

Generally, it is recommended to study Gann's works in the order in which he wrote them. All of his books present trading tools and ideas that can be directly applied to the markets. However, I am going to focus primarily on *How to Make Profits Trading in Commodities,* since it is the book my father first handed me when introducing me to Gann's works.

I asked my father why he chose this particular book, and he said that it was because he had come to learn that it clearly delineated rules pertaining to a few important topics.

- The first was that of protecting a position in the market through the strategic placement of stop orders.

- The second category was "buying points", the terminology which Gann used to describe patterns to buy into the market, or go long.
- And the third category was "selling points", describing how to sell into the market, or go short.

My father said that the *Commodities* book not only explored these key topics, but also presented many examples to reinforce the stated rules, making it easier to directly apply the concepts to any market.

Of the published books listed above, five open with a portrait of Gann. Every time I see one of those portraits, I feel that his expression conveys the following—"Trading is serious business. Get ready to work hard and come out a more successful trader on the other side."

In *How to Make Profits Trading in Commodities*, the following always jumped out to me in the Foreword, written by Gann himself: "**I do not believe in gambling or reckless speculation**, but am firmly convinced, after years of experience, that **if traders will follow rules and trade on definite indications, that speculation can be made a profitable profession.**"

Right there we have the keys—follow the rules and trade on definite indications. But what comprises that? The chapters ahead will explore those items.

Gann also wrote "Trading in commodities is not a gambling business, as some people think, but a practical, safe business when conducted on business principles." So, you may be wondering, what are Gann's "business principles?" You will discover these in the pages ahead as well.

Focus of This Book

Now that I've introduced you to Gann's works and some of his most memorable forecasts, I want to explore what exactly will be contained in this book. It is very aptly titled on two levels.

The first is in calling it the "Trading" methods of W.D. Gann. From all of the original materials studied by many Gann experts, the methods presented boil down to two categories.

The first is forecasting. Merriam-Webster defines forecasting as "calculating or predicting (some future event or condition) usually as a result of study and analysis of available pertinent data." There are a multitude of forecasting methods which Gann employed, such as measuring angles on his hand-written charts, or using Natural Squares.

These were among the prime tools that he used to make predictions about future market action. However, **how did Gann actually trade the market** when his predictions came true, or ever fell short? THAT is information that I want to explore with you, **so that you can directly apply it to your charts.**

"When" to invest is covered by forecasting tools. But "how" to invest is covered by trading methods, again returning to the title of this book.

The second way that this book is very aptly titled is in mentioning your "technical analysis toolbox." Think about it like this: when you are building a house, you need more than just nails. You need a hammer and boards and a saw, and you need to know how to use them correctly so that you don't cut off a finger or mangle your hand in the process!

You can tackle this book in parts. Learning one tool or method is like having a hammer and nails. And you can do a lot with it, but you can't build a house with just those alone.

One of my first coaching students, Jay I., came to me with a toolbox that was one of the "cleanest" I've ever seen at the start of a mentorship. He knew what tools to use for his NQ futures day trading, but needed my guidance to help hone in on the most powerful tools and let go of the ones that weren't helping to boost his trading account.

Jay's short-term goal was to trade in simulation and then get funded by a prop trading account, and he accomplished that within a month of completing his mentorship! We're still friends and I stay in touch with Jay, hearing the latest updates on the fine trading toolbox that he's built.

So this *Trading Methods of W.D. Gann* book gives you strategies and tools like the ones that worked for Jay. And they tie into my Hima Reddy University (himareddy.com/gannuniversity), where I teach you how to use them together properly to build a Frank Lloyd Wright masterpiece—to build a "house" that produces consistent profits over and over.

The bulk of this book contains many of Gann's trading principles and methods, interpreted through diagrams I've created as well as chart examples.

Towards the end of the book, I'll show you how Gann employed these tools together, and I'll guide you on how to learn more directly from his written works.

I believe that the greatest value in what I've provided is in the individual market case studies. They are all directly applicable to any active market that you choose to trade, and I encourage you to follow along with the details of each example as it is presented.

Download and Print your Companion Guide FIRST, before you dive into the teaching, with full size and full color charts at himareddy.com/gann2bonus

Trading Rules

Some of the other books out there which analyze Gann's works and many of the websites and blogs which touch upon the subject explore an important list of trading rules Gann wrote back in 1949. In *45 Years on Wall Street,* pages 16 and 17 list twenty-four "never-failing" trading rules that were based upon his personal experience.

However, eight years earlier, Gann had published a list of twenty-eight "valuable" rules in *How to Make Profits Trading in Commodities* (page 43). From the list of twenty-eight rules to the list of twenty-four rules, only a few rules were altered due to the focus of the subject matter (stocks versus commodities).

The appendix of this book contains Gann's original twenty-eight rules, incorporating the stock-related edits (see Appendix A). As you can see, many of Gann's rules use negative words such as "never" and "don't" to get his points across. The last of the 28 rules even states "Avoid getting in wrong and out wrong; getting in right and out wrong; this is making double mistakes."

This rule really resonated with me when I first read it. It made me realize that if I could break down the elements of my thoughts and actions (essentially, these rules), I would be more likely to do the one thing Gann wanted his students to do, but that he didn't say out-right—get in (the market) right, and get out right.

In order to focus on correct action, I decided to go through Gann's rules and rephrase any that were written with negative language. Why?

Because I believe that telling my coaching students, especially those that I coach one-on-one, what they should or *can* do is a more effective teaching method than telling them what they shouldn't or *can't* do.

Therefore, the appendix of this book also includes a second list of Gann's rules, but in their "affirmative" form (See Appendix B). I will refer to the "affirmative" rules throughout this book where applicable.

To begin,

Gann Rule (Affirmative) #26: Only follow another man's advice if you know that he knows more than you do.

I'm sharing this rule first to encourage you to explore the rest of this book proactively. I have come to see how Gann's trading methodologies work time and time again, but don't take my word for it. Examine the examples and even observe your own markets of interest to see the knowledge at work.

"I'd like to give great praises for Hima Reddy and the mentorship we just wrapped up. I loved every minute of learning, and Hima's under-promise over-deliver-giving personality.

Over 6 months ago I came across her educational material, it clicked, and I immediately purchased just about everything she offers. I was already trading by then, but knew I could use some fine tuning and adjustments.

When I got offered 1on1 mentoring, it was a no brainer, even if I had to scrape up for funding, it was totally worth investment. My goal was to be able to make 1K in a day, NQ,1 contract. The adjustments she made to my trading plan, and fine tuning my understanding of the charts, changed my trading skills forever.

Being able to email personally, get questions answered, clarifications on a sticking point, and repetitiously watch her break down her chart analysis has made me a better trader. Hima, you're not just one of my fav mentors, you're one of my favorite ppl on earth with a huge heart for teaching and your students. I can't thank you enough. Can't wait till we partner up mentoring again in the future. Thank you always." ~ Jay. I.

---

[1] _The Natural Squares Calculator_ course workbook (Pomeroy: Lambert-Gann, 2002), 10-12.

If you haven't already, Download and Print your Companion Guide with full size and full color charts at himareddy.com/gann2bonus

---

2

Elements of the Market

Basic Market Movement

According to Gann, a trend makes an advance or decline in three to four "sections". Essentially, any bull or bear market run will play out as shown:

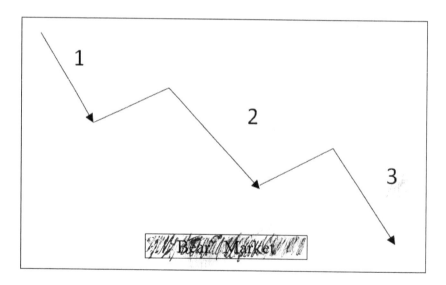

Figure 2.1

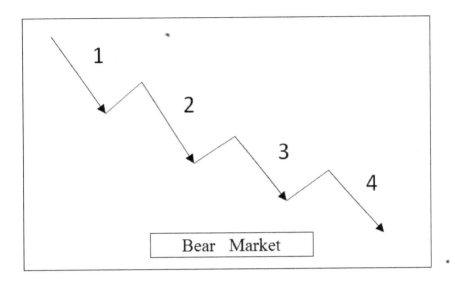

Figure 2.2

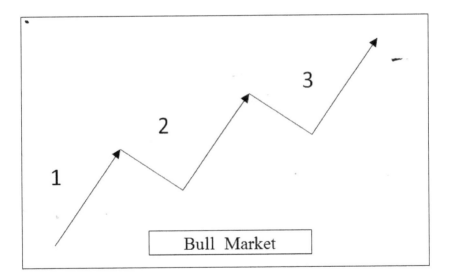

Figure 2.3

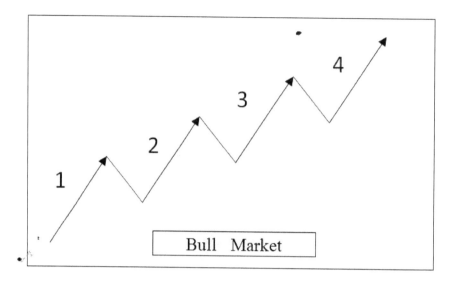

Figure 2.4

Figures 2.1 through 2.4 are NOT drawn to scale and are not measuring any amount of price or time movement—they are just showing the DIRECTION of price movement.

From this point forward, I will present actual Gann methods that you can instantly apply to your study of security price charts. I will give many case studies along the way, and I want you to note a couple of things about the charts.

First, I am plotting OHLC (open high low close) charts in the strong majority of the case studies. OHLC charts are also commonly referred to as bar charts. Gann drew his charts by hand, so nearly all of them are drawn in the OHLC style. Therefore I believed presenting bar charts would be the best way to keep the focus of the case studies on Gann's methods.

I have also plotted price bars in a uniform color (black). You may know that some charting software platforms plot bars in green when the closing prices are above the opening prices, or plot in red for when the closing prices are below the opening prices.

My software, TradeStation, has similar capacities. But for the purpose of studying the tenets in this book, I think it's best to keep it simple. So I will use black price bars against a white background.

Also, new in this second edition book, I have truncated date details to the style my traders and especially my coaching students have become accustomed to in my research and digital education.

 One of my students, Meri G., annotated her charts quite neatly, but there was a bit too much information, distracting her from what she really needed to see. Teaching Meri a variety of my annotation methods, including the way I mark dates on charts and in research, helped clear the cobwebs so she could focus on the key (most important) market action.

Lastly, new in this second edition book, I have included my Jedi momentum indicator, the RSI Power Zones [2], on several chart case studies. I go in-depth into the indicator and how it ties into Gann's methods in my Hima Reddy University to make sure you apply it best.

Now we return to the basic tenets of Gann's works.

Price is King

According to the Oxford Dictionary, the second definition of the word "king" is "a person or thing regarded as the finest or most important in its sphere or group."

This is what I'm getting at when I say "Price is King." It leads many other factors that are present in market analysis, and it is one of the most basic elements that you need to initiate sound, profitable, reliable analysis.

In a true monarchy, the demands of every citizen and the supply of goods and services to meet those demands may weigh back and forth, but ultimately it is the king who has the power to decide who "wins". Similarly, the demand and supply within the context of a market will ebb and flow, but the agreed-upon price is the ultimate rule as to whether buyers or sellers are in the lead.

Price discounts every factor out there that you think may be affecting your trading or investing decisions.

Many people at first find it hard to believe that big news stories or economic data reports can already be accounted for in the price movement, but it is true. It is true simply because everyone with a vested interest in a particular market is acting on that interest by buying, selling, or waiting on the sidelines.

And if they are waiting on the sidelines, no matter how rich or powerful or knowledgeable they might be, they are not influencing price movement, period.

If they are buying or selling, no matter how small a position or no matter what they used to base their decisions, it is the action of the buyers and sellers that reflects all the factors that could be affecting the security. So, when a company's earnings are announced, for example, it is not the information itself that influences the subsequent price movement. It is the traders' REACTIONS to the information that causes any erratic price action to take place.

Examples throughout this book will illustrate the importance of focusing on price when analyzing the markets for a trading opportunity.

Patterns Repeat

The definition of the word "pattern" as explained by Merriam-Webster is "a form or model proposed for imitation". Within the context of the financial markets, a pattern is a reoccurring series of actions.

Why do things reoccur? Why do patterns repeat themselves? One answer for this can be tied to what Gann once wrote—"Everything in existence is based on exact proportion and perfect relation.

There is no chance in nature because mathematical principles of the highest order are at the foundation of all things."[3]

Relating back to price, while it may seem at times that price is moving randomly within a market, there is always a relationship in a move to another.

To illustrate this on the most basic level, let's examine the possibilities of comparisons between charts.

Looking at two securities which have no direct relationship (economic sector, etc.), patterns can and do often repeat.

Take a look at Figure 2.5:

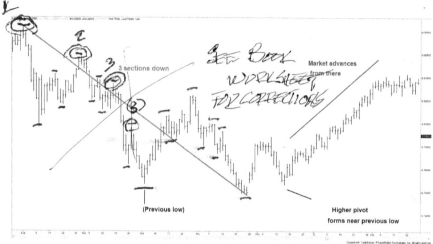

Figure 2.5, NZDUSD, Daily, as of Mar 7, 2012
Created with ©TradeStation Technologies, Inc. All rights reserved.

From Aug 1, 2011 to Nov 25, 2011, NZDUSD (New Zealand Dollar priced in terms of United States Dollars) declined over the course of three sections. A higher pivot (turn) then formed very close to a key previous low former level. The market then rallied from there.

PRIMO CHART

DON'T MISS THE BIG MOVE -
1. PLOT THE PTG-XT "EXTREME INDICATOR
2- IN A "YELLOW BUY BLOCK" BUY THE BAR CLOSE
   < PREVIOUS BARS LOW
3. IN A RED CELL BLOCK" SELL THE BAR CLOSE >
   PREVIOUS BARS HIGH.

Now look at Figure 2.6, another chart of a completely different security:

Figure 2.6, MU, Daily, as of Mar 7, 2012
Created with ©TradeStation Technologies, Inc. All rights reserved.

As Figure 2.6 shows, Micron Technology declined from Apr 27, 2011 to Oct 4, 2011 over the course of three sections. A higher low then formed very close to a key previous low level. Shares rallied from there.

In this comparison, I have combined segments of price movements into relatively large patterns, considering their impact on future price action.

In some cases, this is an extension of the traditional technical analysis treatment. This is because I want to emphasize the point that **any consistently tradable market setup can be considered a pattern.** They are valid entry and exit signals because they have occurred many times in the past and the probability of their outcomes is weighted towards specific scenarios. Keep this in mind as you explore Gann's specific buying and selling points.

In exploring patterns, we've compared two different securities using one time frame. Now, let's keep the security static, and look at consecutive patterns emerging over one time frame.

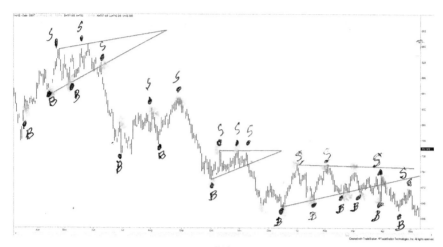

Figure 2.7, WU12, Daily, as of May 3, 2012
Created with ©TradeStation Technologies, Inc. All rights reserved.

Figure 2.7 depicts a daily chart of the Sep 2012 Wheat futures contract. As you can see, a series of converging trade patterns have been delineated. These patterns are tradable not only in terms of watching for the breakdown, but also in being able to monitor trades relative to the boundaries.

For example, within the first pattern delineated towards the top of the chart, as the pattern emerged in real time, one could use Gann's buying points (I'll refer to them as patterns) to enter long positions off the lower boundary of the formation. One could also use Gann's selling patterns to enter short positions from the upper boundary of the pattern.

The exact buying and selling techniques will be explored in Chapter 4: Trading the Market, but what's important here is to understand the significance of patterns as they emerge in markets, and how they add to the tradability of the underlying security.

Lastly, let's look at one security, but over two different time frames to see what patterns emerge within both.

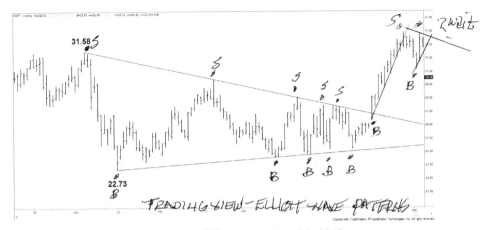

Figure 2.8, MSFT, Weekly, as of Apr 27, 2012
Created with ©TradeStation Technologies, Inc. All rights reserved.

Figure 2.8 shows a weekly chart of Microsoft. Following the decline from $31.58 (Apr 23, 2010 high) to $22.73 (Jul 1, 2010 low), a period of sideways trading commenced. The period of trading took on a triangular, converging form, and a breakout did not appear until the week of Jan 6, 2012.

If you haven't already, Download and Print your Companion Guide with full size and full color charts at himareddy.com/gann2bonus

LANCE / WEALTH PRESS / "MASTER INDICATOR" ON T.O.S.
① ARROWS (GREEN/RED)/PINK ON PRICE CANDLE STICKS
② -LOWER HISTOGRAM Shows SIGNALS - SIGNALS Confirm ARROWS
③ -5, 15, 30, 1 HR, DAILY WEEKLY TIME CHARTS
       (GOOD ON ALL TIME FRAMES)
④ CHECK CCI A160 & CONFIRM MOMENTUM.
★⑤ USE Trading View for Elliott Wave patterns &
     others.
⑥ - USE TRADERS PRO TO VERIFY
⑦ - USE TRADE ALGO
⑧ USE MURRAY MATH
⑨ - USE ACTIVE STRENGTH
⑩ - USE CHAIKEN

Figure 2.9, MSFT, Daily, as of Feb 2, 2012
Created with ©TradeStation Technologies, Inc. All rights reserved.

PULL UP THIS CHART & APPLY ELLIOTT WAVES

Figure 2.9 shows a daily chart of Microsoft, essentially one time frame lower than the prior weekly chart. After the rally from $23.65 (Jun 16, 2011 low) to $28.15 (Jul 26, 2011 high), a period of sideways trading commenced. Interestingly enough, this triangular, converging trading took place within the context of the price action of Figure 2.8. The breakout of the daily pattern coincided with the breakout of the weekly pattern, occurring in the daily chart on Jan 4, 2012.

The goal of these examples is to reinforce the notion that all of the action of price and formation of patterns are **repetitions of mathematical relationships within the markets.** This is why similar patterns emerge in different markets as well as different time frames.
MURRAY MATHEMATICS

Even though I've focused on triangular patterns for these examples, ALL types of patterns repeat in markets. The case studies coming ahead in Chapter 3 will demonstrate that.

The Construct of Time

When reading Gann's books, he references days, weeks, months and years. He does specifically say that the more time "between the top and bottom, the more important it is."

What this means is that the longer a market move endures, whether it's a rally or a decline, the more significant its ending pattern (top or bottom) will be in terms of subsequent price action.

However, as I'll show in real chart examples of specific buying and selling patterns, it is evident that these price and pattern relationships can play out in any active market and on any time frame and for any duration of time. For example, a 5-minute chart of Soybean futures can illustrate the same pattern that one may see on a quarterly (3 months per period) U.S. bond futures chart.

Let's move from "time relative to patterns" back to "time in relation to price".

In order to ultimately master Gann's most advanced techniques, one must accept the following: that **Gann talks about price and time in such similar capacity because they are completely related.** The source of man's time and the source of man's price system are one in the same. Here's a thought process to help you follow what I mean by this statement.

Time, at its most basic level, is a system used to measure our location on Earth in relation to other celestial bodies in the universe.

At 12:00 A.M. midnight on any Jan 1st, we celebrate the passage of one year of time, but really we are celebrating the fact that the Earth has completed one full orbit around the Sun. Over the course of any day, we move through our work, play, and rest according to the hands of a clock that we (human beings) invented, but that is just our attempt at measuring something which exists whether we measure it or not!

The planets do not rotate on axes or move about the sun (and each other) because we measure time. It is actually the other way around—man has developed the system of timekeeping to account for such movements through space. If you've ever looked at a calendar or clock and utilized what you saw to make decisions in your life, then you have directly related your life's actions to the movements of the planet you inhabit and the celestial bodies that surround it.

Now let's think about price.

Again, it is a "man-made" measurement of the value of some entity. Relative to our study, it is the measurement of the value of an object (a stock share, a futures contract, etc.). This value is derived from the supply and demand for the object. The supply and demand is based in human wants and needs, and these rise and decline in direct relation to human psychology and emotions.

All prices are reflections of the complete value that humans give to objects. Since all humans operate within the created context of time, price is directly linked to time.

This can be hard for students new to the markets to grasp. Why? Because we are taught that *humans* create. In reality, we don't create anything new, we only recreate and re-present things which have already been presented to us and/or are at our disposal. As you continue your exploration of Gann's works, what I'm saying will make more and more sense.

So, accepting that price and time are essentially one in the same, if "price is king", time rules right by its side. The two axes of any security chart involve price and time, and so long as you study these two measurements, you can use Gann's methods to make more accurate and successful trades and investments.

 This breakthrough really helped one of my earliest coaching students, Robert P. In order to improve his forecasting using my simplest market timing tools, we worked on getting him to look at BOTH axes on the chart with equal weight and importance.

Robert's identification of cycles improved greatly! And by the end of his mentorship Robert was able to be ready for the highest probability trade setups in the SPY and swing trade them by honing into the key market timing windows.

Once again, time has now been revealed as a construct of sorts. Therefore, it may not be so difficult for you to understand that no matter what chart time frame is used to plot a security's price data, the effectiveness of price-based trading methods *will not* alter.

Figure 2.10, GOOGL, Weekly, as of Sep 4, 2009
Created with ©TradeStation Technologies, Inc. All rights reserved.

Figure 2.10 examines a weekly chart of Google. The company's initial public offering took place on Aug 19, 2004. The uptrend off the low placed that day at $95.96 extended for over 3 years, reaching a high of $747.24 (Nov 7, 2007) before a severe downturn occurred.

Figure 2.11, GOOGL, Daily, as of Mar 3, 2011
Created with ©TradeStation Technologies, Inc. All rights reserved.

Figure 2.11 looks at the daily price action of the same stock. The chart shows that price movement similar to that displayed in Figure 2.10 occurred off the new major low that was posted at $247.30 (Nov 21, 2008).

Figure 2.12, GOOG, 60 minutes, as of Feb 8, 2011
Created with ©TradeStation Technologies, Inc. All rights reserved.

Moving on to the intraday level, Figure 2.12 presents an instance where the same type of price action showed itself on the 60-minute chart.

What does this demonstrate?

The rules of price action are the same *no matter* what time frame you are observing.

The same price movements that occur on a weekly chart of a security can occur on another time frame of that same security. The point/dollar range of the moves may differ between time frames since the larger the time frame, the more data is captured. But the structures of the price action will be the same.

As you observe multiple securities over time, you will see how often similar price developments continue to present themselves within the same security over multiple time frames.

Some of what I shared relating to Price, Patterns, and Time may seem redundant. That's because these three elements connect on many different levels and the only way to absorb these relationships is to study examples over and over again.

Take these ideas to your own market observation and keep track of the relationships you uncover. They will strengthen your understanding of how the basic elements of the market move together to create one seamless representation of a security's activity.

"Thank you for your intuitive understanding of my needs in trading. I see the importance of building upon a simple, basic foundation. I can hardly wait to start implementing your recommended strategies!"
– Meri G., Washington

[2] You can find out more about my RSI Power Zones at himareddy.com/myrsi as that is beyond the scope of the work covered here :)

[3] *How to Make Profits Trading in Commodities*, W.D. Gann 1941

If you haven't already, Download and Print your Companion Guide with full size and full color charts and get your Video Walkthroughs at himareddy.com/gann2bonus

PRO TRADER STRATEGIES - overlooked Tool.
(cents to $500)

- Buying (inexpensive stocks) before they take off
  A. Dynamic Stop levels - A proprietary stop placement formula that moves with the "ebb and flow" of price and is specifically designed to track the behavior of the market you are currently trading.
- "Dynamic stops" can keep you in a winning trade as long as possible.
- There are also other advantages to trading with the new Dynamic Stop levels
- Use 2 to 6 EMA's (white yellow, yellow/black) to determine your turn over point.
- Also use Primo Oscillator to confirm along with Hima Red.

3

Interpreting the Market

Gann's View of Price Movement

This chapter begins with an exercise to connect you with Gann's most foundational views on how price fluctuates. It may be a bit rudimentary for a seasoned analyst. But it never hurts to take a fresh look at something one has been familiar with for so long. For the reader newer to price charts and Gann's works, I believe this will provide an excellent way to get started.

Settle down with a blank sheet of paper and a pencil for the following exercise:

- First, draw a horizontal line just above the bottom of the paper, all the way across.
- Second, draw a vertical line just inside the right edge of the paper.

Your sheet of paper should now look something like Figure 3.1.

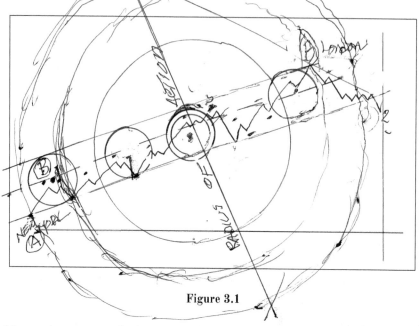

Figure 3.1

Now, picture a stock chart. Close your eyes to gather the details of the image you see for a few moments. Then open your eyes.

Take the image that you had in your mind's eye and roughly sketch it out on the paper, remaining above the horizontal line and to the left of the vertical line that you had already sketched.

What does your stock chart image look like?

- One possibility is jagged lines with high points and low points.
- Another is a gentle curve.
- It could be a steadily rising line with minor high points and low points along the way.

Most people envision price charts with smaller segments that connect within a bigger picture. However, if you pictured and drew a relatively straight line, that's fine too.

Bring your attention back to your drawing, and focus on the first data point on your chart. This is most likely going to be the first mark you drew towards the left side of your paper. This would represent the first point marking a traded price, relating to the vertical line (representing the price axis) and a specific time, relating to the horizontal line (representing the time axis). **Label this point A.**

Move your eyes towards the right side of the paper.

- If point A is lower than the points that follow it, move towards the right to find the immediate next high point, and label that high point as B.
- If point A marks a high, find the immediate next low that appears after it and label that B.
- If the data points in your drawing are clustered close together, just jump ahead to find a second point.

All that matters is that the second point you move to is the end of a move (or section), whether higher or lower, off of the first point. **And you should only have two points marked: A and B.**

Looking at the path from point A to point B, what would you say is the most significant location between the two? Let's move to a real-life analogy to help us zone in on the answer. This explanation really helped the concept "click" for my coaching student Elaine C., who focused on swing trading futures, and it can be adapted for any market on any time frame.[4]

Imagine that you are a pilot commanding a plane which intends to travel from New York to London. You would have to be aware of the distance to be covered on the journey, the amount of fuel required to complete it, and whether your plane has that amount of fuel. Another point to be aware of is the radius of action.

According to the *Oxford English Dictionary*, the radius of action is a technical term in air navigation used to refer to the point on a flight at which, due to fuel consumption, a plane is no longer capable of returning to the airfield from which it originated. Given the path from New York (point A) to London (point B), what would be the radius of action? *50% OF DISTANCE*

Presuming that the fuel levels had been adjusted to be able to cover this journey precisely, the radius of action would be the halfway point of the distance from New York to London.

- If your plane were to come up to the halfway point of the journey, it would still have enough fuel reserved to turn around and return to New York successfully.
- However, if the plane were to pass through the halfway point, the remaining amount of fuel would be less than what was used to cover the initial leg of the journey.

In this case the plane would NOT be able to turn around and come back to New York after travelling through the halfway point to London.

Back to the path on the stock chart from point A to point B: what is the most significant location between the two? You may not know offhand. You may think there are an infinite number of points from which to choose. Or, still following the analogy to the radius of action, you may say "The halfway point!" *MURRAY MATH LINES 0-50%/50-100% 4/8 4/8 to 8/8 ths*

Returning to the line segment as part of a stock chart, the market may rest if the halfway point between A and B is not surpassed, and may *return* towards A before any second attempt toward B is made. As described here, in geometry terms, the midpoint (middle point) equally divides a line segment into two equal parts. In fraction terms, it is the ½ point. In percentage terms, it is 50%.

Using percentage terms, let's revisit points A and B. Let's give the A anchor point a value of 0, and the B anchor point a value of 100. With this setup, the 50% level equals 50 in value as well as in percentage terms.

- Draw a dashed horizontal line through A (0) and another horizontal line (which will be parallel) to B (100).
- Draw a dashed horizontal line through the 50% level between these two points.

You now have a segment of space located between the 0 line and the 50% line, and another segment of space between the 50% line and the 100 line.

Looking at these two new segments of space created by finding the 50% level between A and B, you can divide each space once again. The midpoint of 0 to 50 is 25.

- Draw a horizontal line equidistant from the 0 line and the 50% line to represent 25%. The midpoint of 50 to 100 is 75.
- Draw a horizontal line equidistant from the 50% line and the 100 line to represent 75%.

There are now three special markers on the road from A to B; 25, 50, and 75.

Now divide one last time. The midpoint of 0 to 25 is 12.5.

- Draw a horizontal line equidistant from the 0 line and the 25% line to represent 12.5. The midpoint of 25 to 50 is 37.5.
- Draw a horizontal line equidistant from the 25% line and the 50% line to represent 37.5%. The midpoint of 50 to 75 is 62.5.
- Draw a horizontal line equidistant from the 50% line and the 75% line to represent 62.5%. Lastly, the midpoint of 75 to 100 is 87.5.

- Draw a horizontal line equidistant from the 75% line and the 100% line to represent 87.5%.

Your paper should now look like Figure 3.2

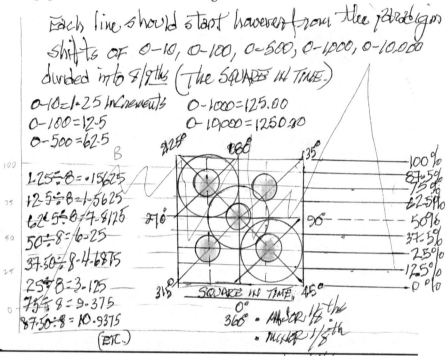

Figure 3.2

Congratulations! You've just uncovered eighths retracement levels. Gann was the first to write about using eighths retracements for market analysis and trading.

A retracement in a market is a correction within the context of the greater trend. In an uptrend, a retracement is a corrective move lower before high prices are seen. In a downtrend, a retracement is a corrective move higher before lower prices are seen.

The percentage levels created when breaking down a move into eighths are 0, 12.5, 25, 37.5, 50, 62.5, 75, 87.5, and 100. One can also measure retracements as fractions (0, 1/8, 2/8, 3/8, etc.).

Either way, these retracement levels are all key areas to watch for a resumption of the existing trend when a retracement is in place, or the beginning of a change of trend.

The 50% level of any move is the most significant area to consider as a potential turning point of the price action. A change in price direction would be likely if the market ever approaches, precisely touches, or pokes through, and bounces from that level.

Respecting the 50% level on a dip down within a steadily rising market will create a price floor, or "**support**". Respecting the 50% level on a rally within a steadily falling market will create a price ceiling, or "**resistance**".

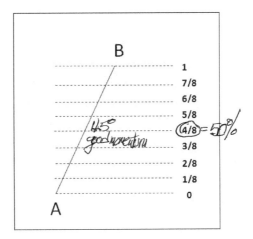

Figure 3.3

Figure 3.3 illustrates eighths retracements. The support and resistance levels are derived from a specific segment of market action. During the drawing exercise, you looked closely at a move from a price point A to a price point B, but the subsequent moves to a point C, a point D and onwards would provide the other derivations of support and resistance, as shown in Figure 3.4.

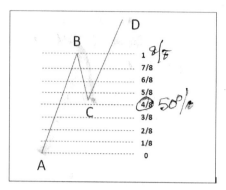

Figure 3.4

Projections Based on Existing Price Movement

Referring back to the statement that every move is mathematically re-lated to another, as you can plainly see on any security chart, there are many different moves that make up the flow of a market.

For example, a section higher in an uptrend on a weekly chart can be viewed in smaller segments on a daily chart, consisting of sections higher as well as corrections lower. The moves themselves may occur within a clear uptrend, clear downtrend, or in a non-trending situation.

So, how does one ultimately determine what move or moves to use to project future price action? Remember back to the AB segment noted on your sketch of stock market action. If AB is an advance from a low point A to a high point B, this is recognized as a section upwards. If a downward correction begins from point B, it is primarily taking place as a reaction to the preceding move. Wherever the correction ends can be labeled point C. When the uptrend resumes, you will have a couple ways to project price action.

The first is to calculate the new strength only in relation to the initial first section's up. To give you the correct visual, Figure 3.5 shows what the A-B-C move might look like, with eighths retracements overlaying it:

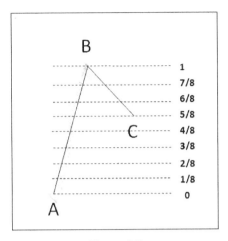

Figure 3.5

Figure 3.6 takes the entire set of eighths retracements and projects them out from point B.

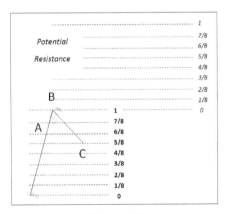

Figure 3.6

If you apply this method of projections to any of your charts, you will start to uncover which primary sections are capturing the rhythm of that market. And you will come to see that the projected resistances are useful in uncovering price targets.

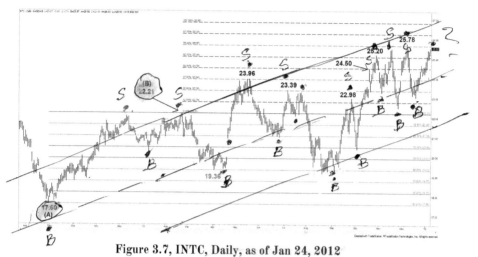

Figure 3.7, INTC, Daily, as of Jan 24, 2012
Created with ©TradeStation Technologies, Inc. All rights reserved.

Figure 3.7 illustrates this method of retracement projection using a chart of Intel. The initial set of retracements was drawn from $17.60 (Aug 31, 2010), low point A, up to $22.21 (Feb 18, 2011), high point B. After retracing to $19.36 (Apr 4, 2011 low), which was just over 19.33, the 62.5% retracement, the stock resumed its uptrend and broke higher. The projection of the initial set of retracements was added onto the chart.

The projected retracements provided several useful points of resistance over the next eight months.

1. The high at $23.96 (May 18, 2011) tested the projected 37.5% retracement at 23.94.
2. The lower high at $23.39 (Jul 7, 2011) tested the projected 25% retracement at 23.36.
3. The $22.98 high (Sep 27, 2011) pierced the projected 12.5% retracement at 22.79.
4. Continuing higher, the $24.50 high (Oct 19, 2011) approached the projected 50% retracement at 24.52.
5. The $25.20 high (Oct 27, 2011) tested the projected 62.5% retracement at 25.09.

6. And lastly, of the projected retracement levels shown, the $25.78 high (Dec 7, 2011) posted after a test of the projected 75% retracement at 25.67.

The second method to project future price action from the A-B-C pattern is to calculate new strength in relation to the initial first section up *as well as* the correction itself. One would take the entire set of eighths retracements and project them out from point C. Figure 3.9 illustrates this method.

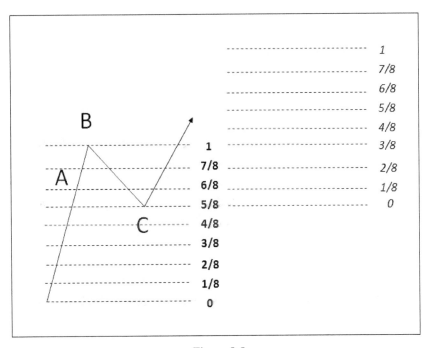

Figure 3.8

Figure 3.9, AUDUSD, Weekly, as of Jan 20, 2012
Created with ©TradeStation Technologies, Inc. All rights reserved.

This weekly chart of AUDUSD (Australian Dollar/U.S. Dollar) illustrates this second method of retracement projection. The initial set of retracements was drawn from $0.6008 (Oct 27, 2010), low point (A), up to $0.9405 (Nov 16, 2009), high point (B). The market corrected to $0.8067 (May 25, 2010 low), probing the 37.5% retracement at 0.8131. The market then proceeded higher, and a set of retracements was projected from the $0.8067 pivot low. Once the market broke out above the $0.9405 swing high, the projected retracements provided resistance, showing that the rhythm of the A-B-C move remained in play.

· $1.0182 (Nov 5, 2010 high) approached the projected 62.5% retracement at 1.0189.

· 1.0256 (Dec 31, 2010 high) then pierced the 1.0189 projected retracement level.

· 1.1011 (May 2, 2011 high) approached the projected 87.5% retracement at 1.1038.

· $1.1080 (Jul 27, 2011 high) probed above the 1.1038 projected retracement level.

Either of these methods of projecting retracement levels can also be used to project support. However, given that prices have a floor at zero, the usefulness of projected retracement support will depend upon how high the level is from which prices are being projected.

Now, for the third method or approach, I'll explore the predominant manner in which I've applied Gann's eighths since writing the first edition of this book.

Take a look at this chart of Apple stock. It's part of a series of three charts as you'll see, but I want to move through step-by-step.

Figure 3.10, AAPL
Created with ©TradeStation Technologies, Inc. All rights reserved.

I've created what I call a set of Gann projections using three points of price action. I apply the Fibonacci projection tool located within my TradeStation charting platform. But instead of using Fibonacci numbers, I entered in the projected percentage levels that you can see here, in this case ranging from 87.5% to 200%.

I highlighted three points on the subsequent Apple price action. Point 1 shows when Apple traded up to the 87.5% projection at 133.37. Price formed a high at 134.54.

This shows the great value of this method. Months ahead of the actual price high forming, it allowed me to have an expectation of when Apple might make a substantial long-term high.

Moving on to point 2, I highlighted this level because it was the 150% projection of the initial set of moves. Generally, **the multiples of 50% are the most important levels** to observe when applying Gann projections. So this would include 100%, 150%, and the 200% projection.

In this example, the 150% projection at 189.34 led to a pause in the price action, but not to the formation of a substantial long-term high.

Lastly, look at point 3. The 200% projection lies at 234.11. And, on Oct 3, 2018, price capped at 233.47. The projected level of resistance at 234.11 was only 0.27% beyond the actual high that formed at 233.47.

Take that in for a moment: many months prior to price action reaching the projected resistance levels, we were able to box in the potential price points for a stock high, with only a 0.27% margin on the most significant peak.

This application of Gann projections can stand alone, but **when you layer projections that are calculated off different sets in a marke**t, all going in the same trend direction, **you can really amplify the utility of this approach** to uncovering potential support or resistance.

Figure 3.11, AAPL

See here that I have now presented a chart of Apple that has an entirely different set of projections that only could have been observed after the first set of projection anchors (highs and lows in price) were in place.

Note that the 55.01 origin point for this set of calculations is the same as the anchor point for the prior set of projections that we analyzed.

On this second chart I have added in label markers 4, 5 and 6.

- Point 4 shows price encountering resistance at the 112.5% projection at 178.94.

- Point 5 shows price stalling after reaching the 125% projection at 188.88. Where things get most interesting is at point 6.

- Point 6, the 175% projection of this move is at 228.65. Recall that the 200% projection of the prior set of calculations was at 234.11.
  Therefore, by layering these projection calculations, zones of projected resistance start to emerge.

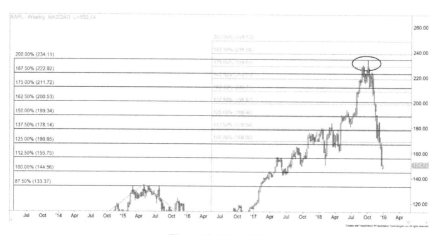

Figure 3.12, AAPL
Created with ©TradeStation Technologies, Inc. All rights reserved.

This third chart shows both sets of projected resistance levels in play. Look at the oval that is marking both the original 234.11 projected resistance level, as well as the 228.65 projected resistance level. On Sep 5, 2018, prices first stopped at 229.67. This is just .44% beyond the projected resistance level at 228.65. Then, the multi-month high came in at 233.47.

These Apple projections have guided my analysis of this stock for years. Not just days or weeks or months, but *years*.

This Gann eighths projection technique can be applied to any active market on any time frame. However, as with any other set of calculations, the greater the timeframe, the greater the potential impact of the projected resistance levels.

You now have an understanding of the most basic ways Gann discovered support and resistance in his markets. As you practice measuring retracements as well as projecting retracements and pure price projections, you will get a feel for how to apply these tools most effectively.

If you would like to view these charts larger and in full color, then please go to himareddy.com/gann2bonus to download your Companion Guide.

Gann and Short Selling

Gann Rule (Affirmative) #18: Be just as willing to sell short as you are to buy. Let your object be to keep with the trend and make money.

In the early pages of Gann's *Truth of The Stock Tape*, he wrote "the general public do not sell stock short". This got me thinking about the idea of short selling.

I remember asking my dad if it was wrong, immoral, "Un-American" to short stock. Because in my initial view, taking such an action would mean that I was essentially rooting for the underlying company to perform poorly.

My dad pondered, then answered. "Markets rise and fall. And they generally fall faster than they rise. If you decide to partake in that action as a short seller, meaning you are selling borrowed shares, then someone needs to buy from you to fulfill the trade. And guess what? Every time you buy stock, someone must sell it to you.

"Stocks will go up or down whether we short them, or not. We can't stop that from happening. **As traders, our job is to extract profits from market moves.** So, to do our job best, we must be willing to go long or sell short as the market dictates per our systems and rules."

How does this tie in with this section on projections and retracements?

Well, consider the AAPL example again. The exercise of calculating projected support can be completed if price action was trending lower instead of higher. But downward trend movement by design, for stocks, generally includes past price history, with significant highs and lows. So using Gann projections for finding support is a bit more redundant. Because the significance of those old highs and lows would be greater than the significance of any projected support levels anyway.

Retracements would be more useful than Gann projections when analyzing a downtrend in price. One exception to this rule is the study of futures charts. If studying the singular front month contract of an active futures contract, Gann projections of potential support can be very helpful.

Gann Eighths Versus Fibonacci Numbers

Earlier in this book, I mentioned that I had surveyed my traders for what they wanted to see when updating this manuscript. One question came in asking "Did Gann use Fibonacci (fans and time scale) for trading?"

While it's difficult to know for sure because we cannot ask Gann directly, here's my take on it. This take is directly from a conversation I had with a trader who heavily applies Gann's work to his trading and analysis.

"Do you think Gann used Fibonacci analysis in his trading and analysis?"

"Well, do you think Gann was aware of Fibonacci numbers?"

"Yes, I do. How could he not have been? Fibonacci numbers had been around for hundreds of years (at a minimum)."

"Ok. We know that Gann liked to put his stamp on things, if you will. So, my theory is that while he was aware of the Fibonacci number sequence and corresponding ratios, and may have even used them, the use of eighths retracements was Gann's own unique spin.

Remember, Gann was analyzing the markets without the speed of computers. Calculating eighths would therefore be much easier than calculating Fibonacci levels, when limited to doing the math by hand or on paper."

Really, I think that it's hard for many of us to understand the incredibly large amount of time it likely took for Gann to update his thousands of paper charts that he used for trading analysis. I have seen these several times with my own eyes.

Therefore, I stand by the hypothesis that, yes, he did use Fibonacci numbers, or knew about them, but that he leaned strongly towards using eights retracement because they were much easier to calculate and provided very similar values in the end.

"This is by far the best material on W.D. Gann, written by a practicing trader and technical analyst. Hima Reddy delivers a simple, direct, and very straightforward approach to Gann analysis. **This book is a necessary addition to a serious trader/technician's toolbox.**" – B. Alden

[4] Video Walkthrough: Plotting Points A and B

If you would like to view these charts larger and in full color, you can Download and Print your Companion Guide and get your Video Walkthroughs at himareddy.com/gann2bonus

FIND SCANNING (APRIL 2023)
- Scans that identify the best markets/sectors to trade.
- Scans that identify the best stocks to trade.
- New Scanning Research
- New Scanning Techniques
- Numerous Scanning COMBINATIONS TO SCAN FROM.

(NEW STRATEGY #7)
ADVANCED SCANNING
CLASS

4

Trading the Market

Trend Assessment and Signal Observation

As I've observed market movement and made trades over the years, I have come to discover that each trade has a lifespan of its own. I broke this lifespan down into eight distinct phases:

1. Trend Assessment
2. Signal Observation
3. Risk Assessment
4. Placement of Orders
5. Trade Initiation
6. Management of Trade
7. Trade Exit
8. Review

This chapter will explore I. Trend Assessment and II. Signal Observation and we will cover the rest in subsequent chapters.

Trend Assessment is the process of determining whether buyers or sellers are in command of the market. The illustrations of sections earlier in this book present a rough idea of how these trends develop.

- An **uptrend** is made up of higher price lows and higher price highs.
- A bull campaign, as Gann wrote, is a long-term uptrend (years in length)
- A **downtrend** is made up of lower price highs and lower price lows.
- A bull campaign, as Gann wrote, is a long-term uptrend (years in length)

As trends unfold and change, traders are able to profit consistently by recognizing buying and selling opportunities. However, **all patterns to buy or sell are not equal.**

Gann makes it very clear in his works that certain buy signals or sell patterns, or "buying points" and "selling points", as he sometimes wrote, are more important than others.

Therefore, I will introduce you to several of Gann's explicit buying and selling patterns relative to their order of importance, which I've come to ascertain through repeated study.

Years ago, when I first read Gann's books and was trying to make his methodologies "my own", I realized that I had a very graphic brain and would best embrace the points presented if I could translate them into illustrations.

So, I read and studied the rules, drew the figures, and collected examples of how the signals worked in real time—on my securities and time frames. In this chapter I will revisit my exercise in illustrating some of Gann's buying and selling patterns.

The exact buying and selling patterns that I will quote come from pages 39 through 41 of Gann's book *How to Make Profits Trading in Commodities.* They are also listed in the appendix of this book (see Appendix C).

The examples used will be marked with text directly relating back to Gann's pattern descriptions.

There are several Affirmative Gann rules to share at this point which will help you keep your focus on the right path as you explore the patterns and case studies:

Gann Rule (Affirmative) #7: Trade only in active markets.

By this, I believe that Gann was advising to trade in markets that have active participation. When you put on a trade you want to be sure that your order can be filled based on the market's volume (or open interest).

Gann Rule (Affirmative) #5: Trade with the trend. Only buy or sell if you are sure of the trend according to your chart and rules.

Gann Rule (Affirmative) #17: Trade only when you have definite signals.

Gann Rule (Affirmative) #12: Trade the swings in accordance with the existing trend. This is where you can make the most profit for the least number of trades.

Gann Rule (Affirmative) #19: Buy only when you have definite indication of a rising market. Sell only when you have definite indication of a falling market.

Gann Rule (Affirmative) #18: Be just as willing to sell short as you are to buy. Let your object be to keep with the trend and make money.

These five rules are all about tuning yourself in to what the market is telling you. Know the trend (dominant market direction). Know the patterns for buying and selling. When they fall into place and you have a "definite indication", that is the time to trade.

The buying and selling points will be presented in several categories. Again, I am sharing these in what I believe to be the order of descending importance.

Reminder: the security examples in this chapter are in bar chart form by design. Bar charts are extremely useful for viewing price action that's developing as well as the underlying forces behind the price action. And using bar charts is an exercise in focusing your attention. By learning these patterns off bar charts, you will be able to more easily identify the patterns when they appear on any type of price chart.

Exceeding Moves in Time

Gann Buying Point #4: "BUY when the first rally from the extreme bottom exceeds in time the greatest rally in the preceding Bear Campaign."

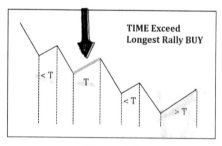

Figure 4.1

The variable "T" stands for "time". T represents the duration of the greatest rally in the Bear Campaign shown. "< T " shows that the other rallies in the decline did not last for as long as rally T.

The signal to look for is when the rally off the low (after a three-section or four-section Bear Campaign) takes more time to develop than T, hence the annotation"> T". This pattern is called TIME Exceed Longest Rally BUY.

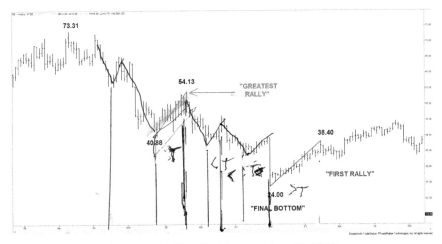

Figure 4.2, PBI, Weekly, as of Apr 12, 2002
Created with ©TradeStation Technologies, Inc. All rights reserved.

Figure 4.2 shows Pitney Bowes on a weekly time frame. The decline from $73.31 (Apr 27, 1999 high) to $24.00 (Dec 16, 1999 low) consists of many rallies, large and small. Let's look at the size of each rally in terms of time, in other words each rally's duration.

- The "greatest rally" occurred when the market rose from $40.88 (Dec 16, 1999 low) to $54.13 (Mar 2, 2000 high), spanning 12 weeks.
- The "first rally" from $24.00 reached $38.40 (Feb 15, 2001 high) before any substantial pullback took hold.

The duration of this "first rally," at 20 weeks, clearly exceeded the greatest rally in the preceding Bear Campaign.

Gann Selling Point #4: "SELL after the first decline exceeds the greatest reaction in the preceding Bull Campaign or the last reaction before final top."

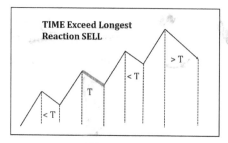

Figure 4.3

To keep this Selling Point in line with the similar Buying Point, I'll focus on the "greatest" reaction (as opposed to the last reaction). The variable T represents the duration of the greatest correction lower within the Bull Campaign shown. "< T" shows that the other corrections in the advance did not last for as long as correction T.

The signal to look for is when the decline from the high (after a three-section or four-section bull campaign) takes more time to develop than T, hence the annotation "> T". This pattern is called TIME Exceed Longest Reaction SELL.

PRIMO STRATEGY #2
(Confirm with REDDY)
• Designed to generate signals in only the strongest of markets
• Applies a proprietary Filtering Process
• Designed to trade quick 5-10 Bar Trades.
• Can apply to Option Trading.
• Aggressive & Conservative Versions.
• Consistency.

Figure 4.4, GOOGL, Daily, as of Sep 3, 2010
Created with ©TradeStation Technologies, Inc. All rights reserved.

Figure 4.4 revisits the Google chart explored earlier in Chapter 2. The rally from $247.30 (Nov 21, 2008 low) to $629.51 (Jan 4, 2010 high) consists of many corrections, small and large. Looking at the size of each correction in terms of time, the "greatest reaction" occurred when the market fell from $447.34 (Jun 5, 2009 high) to $395.98 (Jul 7, 2009 low), spanning 32 days.

The "first decline" from $629.51 reached $520.00 (Feb 25, 2010) before any substantial correction took hold. The duration of this "first decline," at 52 days, clearly exceeded the greatest reaction in the preceding Bull Campaign in *time*.

The next pair of buying and selling patterns focuses on the final rally/reaction in the preceding trend move.

Gann Buying Point #5: "BUY when the period of time exceeds the last rally before extreme lows were reached. "If the last rally was 3 or 4 weeks, when the advance from the bottom is more than 3 or 4 weeks, consider the trend has turned up and commodities are a safer buy on a secondary reaction."

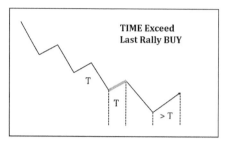

Figure 4.5

The variable T represents the duration of the final rally in the Bear Campaign shown. The signal to look for is when the rally off the low (after a three-section or four-section Bear Campaign) takes more time to develop than the latest rally, hence the annotation "> T". This pattern is called TIME Exceed Last Rally BUY.

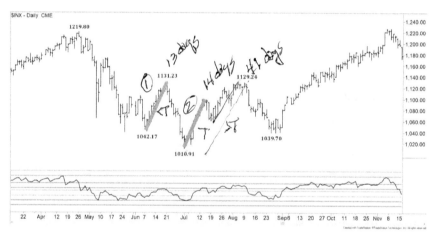

Figure 4.6, $INX, Daily, as of Nov 16, 2010
Created with ©TradeStation Technologies, Inc. All rights reserved.

Figure 4.6 displays the S&P 500 Cash Index. The market declined from 1219.80 (Apr 26, 2010 high) to 1010.91 (Jul 1, 2010 low). The first leg of the rally from the 1010.91 low lasted 13 calendar days. This was akin to the previous rally from 1042.17 (Jun 8, 2010 low) to 1131.23 (Jun 21, 2010 high) which lasted 14 days.

However, the market continued rising off 1010.91 for a total of 41 calendar days, posting a high at 1129.24 (Aug 9, 2010 high). The 41-day time period exceeded the last rally before extreme lows were reached (14 days).

The market reversed lower from the 1129.24 high, and a secondary reaction came in at 1039.70 (Aug 27, 2010 low), testing 1040.49, the 75% retracement of the 1010.91/1129.24 move up.

Gann Selling Point #6: "Sell when the period of time of the first decline exceeds the last reaction before final top of the Bull Campaign. Example: If wheat or any commodity has advanced for several months or for one year of more, and the greatest reaction has been four weeks, which is an average reaction in a Bull Market, then after top is reached and the first decline runs more than 4 weeks, it is an indication of a change in the minor trend or the main trend. The commodity will be a safer short sale on any rally because you will be trading with the trend after it has been definitely defined."

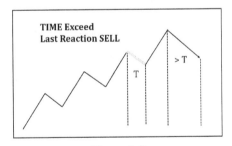

Figure 4.7

The variable T represents the duration of the final correction lower within the Bull Campaign shown. The signal to look for is when the move lower from the high (after a three-section or four-section Bull Campaign) takes more time to develop than the final correction T, hence the annotation "> T". This pattern is called TIME Exceed Last Reaction SELL.

Figure 4.8, CSCO, Weekly, as of Oct 7, 2011
Created with ©TradeStation Technologies, Inc. All rights reserved.

Figure 4.8 shows a weekly chart of Cisco Systems. The market advanced from $13.61 (Mar 9, 2009 low) to $27.74 (Apr 30, 2010 high).

At first, the fall from the $27.74 high lasted 4 weeks. This was akin to the previous reaction from $25.10 (Jan 15, 2010 high) to $22.35 (Jan 28, 2010 low) which lasted 3 weeks.

However, the market continued lower from $27.74 for a total of 10 weeks, posting a low at $20.93 (Jul 1, 2010 low). The time period (10 weeks) had exceeded the "last reaction" before extreme highs were reached (3 weeks).

A reversal from $27.74 was seen to the upside, and a secondary rally came in at $24.87 (Aug 9, 2010 high). Shares declined to $13.30 (Aug 12, 2011) from there.

If you would like to view these charts larger and in full color, then please go to himareddy.com/gann2bonus to download your Companion Guide.

Triple Bottoms/Tops

Gann Rule (Affirmative) #25: Let the market prove it is making a top. Let the market prove it is making a bottom. By following definite rules, you can do this.

Triple Bottoms and Tops (and Double Bottoms and Tops, to be explored) are known and studied within the realm of traditional technical analysis. They are formations that were also very important to Gann and deserve exploration from what I perceived to be *his* point of view through *my* repeated study.

Gann Buying Point #8: "BUY against double or triple bottoms, or buy on first, second or third higher bottom and buy a second lot after wheat, soy beans or cotton makes second or third higher bottom, then crosses previous top."

This Buying Point has several elements to it. I will focus on the Triple Bottom first.

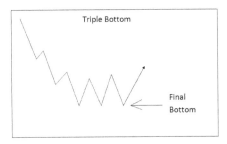

Figure 4.9

The greater the amount of time between the lows of the Triple Bottom, the more significant the following move.

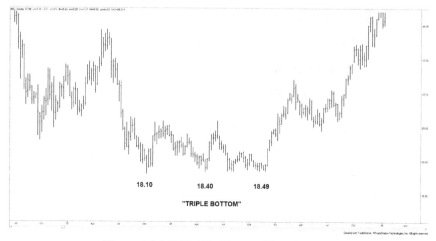

Figure 4.10, RIG, Weekly, as of Dec 3, 2004
Created with ©TradeStation Technologies, Inc. All rights reserved.

Figure 4.10 explores a weekly chart of Transocean, Ltd. The market made a low at $18.10 (Oct 10, 2002). The market then approached the same low, reaching $18.40 on May 1, 2003. Bears attempted to break below that area of support a few months later. The final low was posted at $18.49 (Nov 4, 2003) before the market broke out above the formation.

This example of a Triple Bottom is valuable because it shows a "textbook" version of the formation, in which the peaks in between the lows are also near each other. This is not crucial for the pattern, but it does define a clearer boundary for a breakout.

Another significance of this triple bottom is its duration. The first low to the third low was about 13 months. Remember, **the longer the duration of the topping or bottoming formation, the more significant the subsequent price action**. In this case (not shown on chart), the subsequent advance lasted 30 months, topping at $90.16 (May 11, 2006 high).

Gann Selling Point #8: "SELL against Double Tops or Triple Tops, or SELL when the market makes lower tops or lower bottoms. It is safe to sell when wheat, soy beans, or cotton, makes a second, third, or fourth, lower top, also safe to sell after double and triple bottoms are broken."

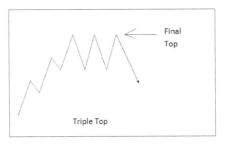

Figure 4.11

Triple Tops tend to be shorter in duration than Triple Bottoms. Why?

Well, to start, a Triple Bottom is a variation of a phase of accumulation. Greed fuels accumulation. A Triple Top, on the other hand, is a variation of a phase of distribution. Fear is the driving force behind distribution. Man's fear is stronger than man's greed.

Fear builds more quickly than greed. Therefore, the lower boundary of a topping pattern such as the Triple Top is likely to be traded through more quickly than the upper boundary of a Triple Bottom.

Now, even though Triple Tops tend to span over less time than Triple Bottoms, time still plays an important role in the analysis of Triple Tops analysis.

As with Triple Bottoms, the greater the amount of time between the highs of a Triple Top, the more significant the following move.

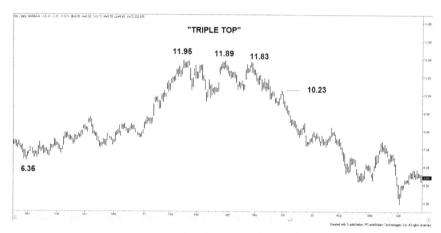

Figure 4.12, MU, Daily, as of Oct 25, 2011
Created with ©TradeStation Technologies, Inc. All rights reserved.

Figure 4.12 revisits the Micron Technology chart explored earlier in Chapter 2. The market made a high at $11.95 (Feb 14, 2011). The market then approached the same high, reaching $11.89 on Mar 30, 2011. The last attempt at that area was seen on Apr 27, 2011, with the high posting at $11.83 before the market tumbled.

This example of a Triple Top is valuable because it shows the variations that can occur within the formation but which still indicate the same bearish sentiment. According to my illustration for a Triple Top, one might expect that all the highs must "match" for the pattern to be valid. However, what's more important is to look at the overall indication of trend that the pattern is painting.

Now let's look at Figure 4.13 which zooms in on the price action of the Triple Top area. Let's walk through each of the indications of this pattern and the subsequent opportunities to go short. Each has its own level of safety, in terms of the risk of the trade not working out. They are labelled as Aggressive, Safer, and Safest.

Figure 4.13, MU, Daily, as of Jun 7, 2011
Created with ©TradeStation Technologies, Inc. All rights reserved.

The first indication that the Final Top within a Triple Top may be forming came on Apr 29, 2011. Shares first broke below higher bar lows at $11.24 (Apr 21, 2011) and $11.25 (Apr 25, 2011). Then shares moved lower before rebounding softly and capping at $11.13 (May 6, 2011).

This would have been an area for an Aggressive sell entry. This is described as aggressive because it is taking action on a pattern that is not yet confirmed, and could see further strength through the original anchor at $11.89 before truly confirming as a topping pattern.

Shares then continued lower towards the $10.26 low (Apr 18, 2011). This was one of the troughs within the pattern of the Triple Top. Therefore, waiting for the break of this low before selling would have been safer than selling based on the earlier break of the $11.24/$11.25 bar lows. The market made its first substantial (closing basis) break below $10.26 on May 17, 2011, and ten shares recovered to $10.21. This would have been an area for a Safer sell entry.

Finally, the last level to watch to confirm the Triple Top was the trough at $9.65 (Mar 10, 2011). Shares broke below this level on May 23, 2011, and continued lower for a couple of days before a rebound took place. The rebound capped at $10.23 (May 31, 2011).

This would have been the area for the Safest sell entry following the Triple Top formation.

Double Bottoms/Tops

Gann Buying Point #8: "BUY against **double** or triple **bottoms...**"

Once again, this Buying Point has several elements to it. I'll now focus on Double Bottoms.

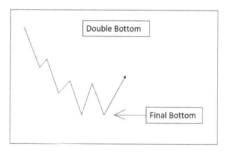

Figure 4.14

Figure 4.15, AMX, Weekly, as of Dec 10, 2010

Figure 4.15 shows America Movil stock on a weekly time frame. The decline from $34.58 (Oct 18, 2007 high) lasted one year, reaching a low of $11.59 (Oct 24, 2008). The market subsequently rebounded to $17.48 (Jan 6, 2009 high). The return move lower reached $11.68 (Mar 2, 2009 low), forming a swing low which was the first indication of a Double Bottom forming. The stock then rallied back through the $17.48 swing high, confirming the Double Bottom pattern.

Note that it took 20 weeks for the Double Bottom to form. The greater the amount of time between the lows, the more significant the low. This became apparent as the advance from the Double Bottom lows extended to last about two years.

Just like how I explained the trade entry points a Triple Top, I will highlight the entry points on this Double Bottom. Look at Figure 4.16 which moves to a daily chart to narrow in on the price action of the Double Bottom area.

Figure 4.16, AMX, Daily, as of Jun 30, 2009
Created with ©TradeStation Technologies, Inc. All rights reserved.

Recall the language used in the first part of explaining the pattern. The word "against" has special meaning. It opens the possibility of trading this pattern even *before* it would be officially confirmed as per traditional technical analysis.

Let's walk through each of the indications of this pattern, this time with the subsequent opportunities to go long, each with their own level of safety in terms of the risk of the trade not working out.

The first indication that the Final Bottom within a Double Bottom may be forming came on Mar 12, 2009. The market broke above the lower bar high at $13.03 (Feb 26, 2009). The market then moved higher before a correction came in, which held at $13.13 (Mar 30, 2009 low).

This would have been an area for an Aggressive buy entry. This is described as aggressive because it is taking action on a pattern that is not yet confirmed, and could see further weakness through the original anchor $11.68 before truly confirming as a bottoming pattern.

 It's important to note that Aggressive buy entries often get accompanied by protective stops that are often "gunned" by market makers. My coaching student Casey C. experienced this often in her short-term futures trading, especially of the ES, NQ, and CL markets, when she first came to work with me in late 2019.

So after building out her trading plan and identifying her strengths and areas for improvement (including stop placement), I prescribed Casey a very clear set of trade management goals to trade in a simulator. Within weeks, she greatly improved her stop placement approach and received "my blessing" to go to live trading! And I continued to demonstrate this over and over in our mentorship group live trading sessions and it really helped turn her trading around.

Returning to AMX, shares then continued higher towards the $15.96 high (Feb 10, 2009). This was swing high within the context of the pattern of the Double Bottom. So waiting for the break of this high before buying would have been safer than buying based on the earlier break of the $13.03 bar high. The market made its first substantial break (closing basis) above $15.96 on Apr 24, 2009, and then shares corrected to $14.94 (Apr 27, 2009). This would have been an area for a Safer buy entry. Why is this considered safer? Because there had been price movement indicating on a fractal level (the trend within the trend) that price is poised to continue higher.

Finally, the last level to watch to confirm the Double Bottom was the peak at $17.48. The market broke above this level on May 4, 2009, and continued higher for a few days before a correction took hold. The correction bottomed out at $17.52 (May 15, 2009). This would have been the area for the Safest buy entry following the Double Bottom formation. This is deemed the safest area because there is no more doubt as to whether the formation is complete.

Note that the market ended up breaking below the $17.52 pivot low to reach $17.39 (Jun 23, 2009 low) before resuming higher.

If you had been long from either one of the $13.13 or $14.94 areas, you would probably have collected your profit and been positioned to re-enter the market long.

If you had gotten long around $17.52, you would have probably taken a small loss and been out of the position.

However, the market always makes it clear when it is giving you a "second chance" to get in on the trend. This is something to keep an eye out for as you apply any of these buying and selling patterns in real time.

Gann Selling Point #8: "SELL against **Double Tops** or Triple Tops...

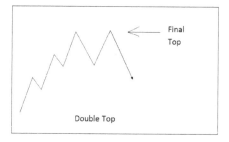

Figure 4.17

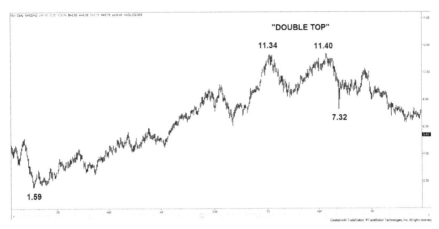

Figure 4.18, MU, Daily, as of Sep 22, 2010
Created with ©TradeStation Technologies, Inc. All rights reserved.

Figure 4.18 looks at the advance in Micron Technology from late 2008 to early 2010. The advance from the $1.59 low (Nov 20, 2008) put in a high at $11.34 (Jan 6, 2010 high). A correction unfolded forming a swing low, but the subsequent rally only reached $11.40 (Apr 4, 2010 high).

This was the first indication that a Double Top may be forming. The break lower to $7.32 (May 6, 2010) confirmed the formation.

As with the Triple Top formation example, there would have been multiple points of entry.

Note that on this daily chart it took three months to form this Double Top, adding to the significance of the pattern in terms of the subsequent downward move.

Figure 4.18.A, TSLA, Daily, as of May 30, 2018
Created with ©TradeStation Technologies, Inc. All rights reserved.

Figure 4.18.A looks at the advance in Tesla from late 2016 to mid-2017. The advance from the $178.19 low (Nov 14, 2016)reached $386.99 (Jun 23, 2017 high). Shares corrected forming a swing low, but the subsequent rally capped at $389.61 (Sep 18, 2017 high).

This is what my late father taught me is a "**test failure**."

A test failure sell signal occurs when a market tests a key resistance level, but within one to two sessions the price closes back beneath that resistance level. The bearish test failure here was the first indication that a Double Top may be forming.

The Nov 2, 2017 gap below $303.13 (Jul 10, 2017 low) confirmed the formation.

Note that in this case the break lower did not lead to a sharp fall in prices. Instead, it was followed by a multi-month rally up to $360.50 (Jan 23, 2018 high) before declines resumed.

Figure 4.18.B, GBPUSD, Daily, as of Sep 5, 2018
Created with ©TradeStation Technologies, Inc. All rights reserved.

To further explore this concept of the test failure, let's look at another Double Top example.

Figure 4.18.B looks at the advance in GBPUSD that initially capped at 1.4333 on Jan 25th, 2018. After pulling back to 1.3711 (Mar 1st, 2018), the currency pair rallied back to the 1.4344 high, but posted a test failure, capping at 1.4376 (Apr 17th, 2018).

This was the first indication that a Double Top may be forming.

Subsequent weakness below the 1.3964 low (Apr 5th, 2018) was the next indication that a Double Top may be in play. And the break back below 1.3711 on May 1st, 2018 confirmed the Double Top pattern.

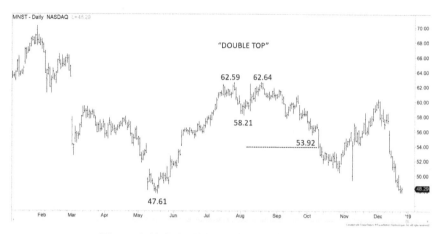

Figure 4.18.C, MNST, Daily, as of Sep 5, 2018
Created with ©TradeStation Technologies, Inc. All rights reserved.

While Double Tops are most commonly associated with forming at the end of extended price uptrends, they can occur at non-extreme levels and be just as effective for trading setups. Figure 4.18.C shows the chart of MNST from a video update I shared on Nasdaq 100 stock components on Sep 12, 2018. [5]

The daily chart shows that price rallied from the low at $47.61 (May 17, 2018) up to the $62.59 (Jul 26, 2018 high). The stock pulled back to $58.21 (Aug 3, 2018 low), then pushed higher.

But once again, here's an example of a test failure at the $62.64 high. Price broke above the $62.59 intraday, but could not post a closing break above that first high. This was the earliest indication that a Double Top might be forming. From there, the stock declined very slowly but steadily.

When I posted my video update on this pattern formation, the Double Top had just recently been confirmed with a break back below $58.21. This is the safest signal to act upon when trading a Double Top pattern. Therefore, in the video I also provided a minimum downside target of $53.92. [5]

This is calculated by taking the height of the Double Top and subtracting that value from the breakdown point of the pattern. The $53.92 target was hit on Oct 10, 2018, about one month after I highlighted the pattern. Note: Trust, but verify!

To see the original video update, please refer to the endnote for the title and then view the video for yourself at himareddy.com/ gann2bonus

Exceeding Moves in Price

Gann Buying Point #3: "SAFEST BUYING POINT. Buy on a secondary reaction after wheat, cotton or any commodity has crossed previous weekly tops and the advance exceeds the greatest rally on the way down from the top."

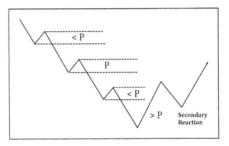

Figure 4.19

Now, it's important to recognize that there are two ways to apply this signal analysis. The first is when price exceeds the size of a previous correction. In future 4.19, the variable P represents the price range in points/cents of the greatest rally in the Bear Campaign shown. So "< P" shows that the other rallies in the decline were not as large as rally P. The signal to look for is when the rally off the low (after a three-section or four-section Bear Campaign) exceeds in size the greatest rally P. The safest time to enter long is once the market has pulled back afterwards, creating a higher low (secondary reaction).

The second examination of the "Exceeding Move in Price" buy signal refers to price action crossing above the most recent top or tops in a downtrend. This is a PRICE Cross Secondary Reaction BUY, and I cover more advanced patterns like these, in-depth in my HimaReddy University, where I can dive deeply with you and make sure you understand these advanced patterns before you deploy them in your trading (himareddy.com/gannuniversity).

Although Gann talks about "weekly" price action, I have come to see how his buying and selling points span all time frames.

Figure 4.20, HON, Daily, as of Feb 7 2012
Created with ©TradeStation Technologies, Inc. All rights reserved.

Figure 4.20 displays a daily chart of the stock Honeywell International. Here, we see that Honeywell declined from the top at $62.28 (May 2, 2011) to the low at $41.22 (Oct 4, 2011). Along the way, the greatest rally took place near the low, from $41.62 (Aug 22, 2011) to $48.45 (Aug 31, 2011). The market crossed the previous top at $48.45 on Oct 12, 2011. The breakout reached a high of $55.81 (Nov 11, 2011) before any major reaction was seen. The safest buying point, the secondary reaction, then came in and found support at $48.82 (Nov 25, 2011), very close to $48.52, the 50% retracement of the $41.22/$55.81 section up.

Gann Selling Point #3: "SAFEST SELLING POINT. Sell on a secondary rally after wheat, soy beans, cotton or any commodity has broken the previous bottoms of several weeks or has broken the bottom of the last reaction, turning trend down. This secondary rally nearly always comes after the first sharp decline in the first section of a Bear Campaign."

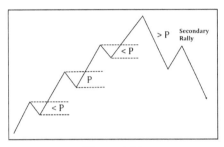

Figure 4.21

Just like with the bullish counterpart to this signal, it's important to recognize that Gann embedded *two* patterns into one description.

The first is a look at when price declines over a larger range of price than it has for the largest move to date within the preceding uptrend. The variable P represents the price range in points/cents of the greatest correction in the bull campaign shown. So "< P" shows that the other corrections during the advance were not as large as correction P. The signal to look for is when the pullback from the high (after a three-section or four-section bull campaign) exceeds in size the greatest correction P. The safest time to enter short is once the market has started to recover, creating a higher low (secondary reaction).

The second examination of the "Exceeding Moves in Price" sell signal refers to price action falling below the most recent bottom or bottoms in an uptrend. This is PRICE Cross Secondary Rally SELL.

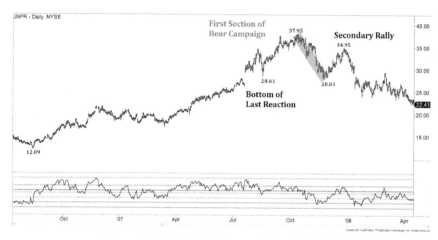

Figure 4.22, JNPR, Daily, as of Apr 15, 2008
Created with ©TradeStation Technologies, Inc. All rights reserved.

Figure 4.22 displays a daily chart of the stock Juniper Networks. Juniper rallied from the bottom at $12.09 (Aug 11, 2006) to the high at $37.95 (October 9, 2007). The last move higher rose from $28.61 (Aug 16, 2007 low), making it the bottom of the last reaction. This level was pierced with the fall to $28.01 on Nov 21, 2007, indicating that bulls were no longer in complete control.

The safest selling point, the secondary reaction, came in at $34.95 (Dec 24, 2007 high). And there's an extra element that can make the safest selling point even safer than what's been described so far. It's the element of market symmetry. This terminology is used within technical analysis outside of Gann analysis. But I have a very specific application for it.

When I talk about **market symmetry**, I am focusing on new highs or lows that match or are symmetrical to previous significant highs or lows. The more recent the old high or low, the more powerful the symmetry impact of the new high or low that forms close to it. This is based on observations that my father and I made on the charts and explanations in several of Gann's books.

Figure 4.23.A CELG
Created with ©TradeStation Technologies, Inc. All rights reserved.

Figure 4.23.A shows the chart of CELG from a video update I shared on Nasdaq 100 stock components on Sep 12, 2018. [5]

There was an advance off the $74.13 low (May 21st, 2018). It capped at $95.30 (Aug 31, 2018 high). Price then broke below the most recent bottom at $89.03 (Aug 23, 2018), stabilizing at $86.33 (Sep 12, 2018). After this price action (and the video update [5]), price turned higher. But it capped out at $92.68. This formed the secondary rally that creates the safest sell opportunity for this pattern.

Now, also notice that $92.68 is in symmetry with the old $93.34 high (Aug 14, 2018). And, these price levels are in symmetry with the old high at $92.96 that had been the start of a steep down move back on Apr 26, 2018. Therefore, even though the $93.34 and $92.96 resistance levels had been violated to the upside with the price action on Aug 31st, there was still useful information to extract from the chart that showed the significance of the $92.68 high when it formed.

> Full disclosure: When I used to make this argument in past professional roles of mine, I would often get my hand slapped, figuratively speaking. There are technicians that believe that once

a support or resistance level had been traded through, it is completely invalid and totally useless going forward.

That is not my experience, though, and in my own study of many Gann charts, I could see the value that he placed on significant old highs and lows. That's why I want to make sure you understand the significance of market symmetry as I see it.

Another aspect of market analysis that is commonly discussed in traditional technical analysis is the fractal nature of markets.

Figure 4.23.B BIIB
Created with ©TradeStation Technologies, Inc. All rights reserved.

Figure 4.23.B shows the chart of BIIB from a video update I shared on Nasdaq 100 stock components on Aug 15, 2018. [6]

Price trended higher, posting a high at $388.67 on Jul 25th, 2018. There was short-term weakness then a gap lower that led to the break below the 339.15 low (Jul 10th, 2018). This was the first indication that the trend may be ending.

Price fell down to $330.90 then stabilized. After recovering to $352.46, price then turned lower again to break below $340.33 (Aug 6th, 2018 low). This illustrates a pattern within a pattern. The first break (below Jul 10th low) provided the framework for a trend reversal.

The second break (Aug 6th low) was fractal in nature and added further evidence to the formation of a top.

Note that in the video [6] I shared two downside targets, 320.14 and 299.73. Both of these targets were met as weakness continued to unfold in line with this PRICE Cross Secondary Rally SELL pattern.

Sometimes the best way to reinforce the significance of a specific price pattern is to illustrate a cautionary tale. Within the same video that reviewed BIIB, I also looked at the chart of REGN. [6]

Figure 4.23.C REGN
Created with ©TradeStation Technologies, Inc. All rights reserved.

In the video, I pointed out that the low at $361.65 (Jul 27th, 2018) was under threat, but I clearly stated that we could get a "test failure" of the support was likely based on current momentum readings. And that's why selling on the break of the support low would not be the safest bet. It would be best to wait for a rebound as the short entry.

This advice proved useful. Price did post a test failure of the $361.65 low, trading down to $361.19 by the end of that Aug 15th session and stabilizing there.

Renewed strength followed that took out the $401.50 high (Aug 2nd, 2018).

So, if you had sold on just the break below the support, then the rally up to $401.50 would have had you thinking you were wrong about an upcoming trend reversal. But you wouldn't have been wrong, you would have been early.

The actual high formed on Aug 30th at $416.49. Tradeable weakness followed that peak.

Now we move on to a brand-new section in this second edition book. It still explores Gann's patterns but does so in what I think is a more intuitive way in terms of how the patterns are classified and named.

To see the original video update, please refer to the endnote for the title and then view the video for yourself at himareddy.com/ gann2bonus

Touches and Pokes

Gann Buying Point #1: "BUY at OLD BOTTOMS or OLD TOP…Buy when.. any commodity.. declines 1c to 3 c under old tops or bottoms."

I have truncated this Buying Point to get to the meat of it and will do so with the relative Selling Point. The full text is present in Appendix C.

The key focus here is to buy (pullbacks to) old tops. But how, exactly? What types of pullbacks are observable, and can be traded? I've named the different scenarios for ease of observation and reference.

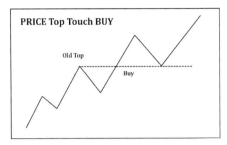

Figure 4.24.A

In Figure 4.24.A the market posts a closing break over a recent high, forming an "Old Top". Then, a pullback "touches" the Old Top. Finally, a turning point (swing low) is formed.

This is the PRICE Top Touch BUY pattern.

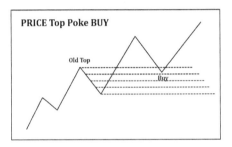

Figure 4.24.B

In Figure 4.24.B, the market falls just below the old top. Depending on how far down the market goes and where it trades from there, this may indicate weakness.

However, if the market turns back above the old top soon after poking above it (less than 25%), this can provide easy-to-find, low-risk opportunities to enter long in an uptrend. This is the PRICE Top Poke BUY Pattern.

Figure 4.24.C GOOGL
Created with ©TradeStation Technologies, Inc. All rights reserved.

On Dec 13, 2017, I published a video update on FAANG stocks. Let's revisit the chart of GOOGL which displayed a PRICE Top Poke BUY pattern. [7]

Figure 4.24.C shows that Google returned to highs at $1008.61 (Jun 6, 2017) and $1006.19 (Jul 24, 2017) on Dec 5, 2017, putting in a low at $1002.32.

From there, the stock soared higher into the following year, peaking at $1198.00 on Jan 29, 2018.

Figure 4.24.D GOOGL
Created with ©TradeStation Technologies, Inc. All rights reserved.

On Jun 27, 2018, I published a video update on FAANG stocks. Let's revisit the chart of GOOGL which displayed a PRICE Top Poke BUY pattern. [8]

Figure 4.24.D shows that Google returned to a high of 1118.15 (May 14, 2018) on date, putting in a low at 1106.07 (Jun 28, 2018). From there, the stock soared higher, peaking at 1291.44 (Jul 27, 2018).

Download and Print your Companion Guide
with full size and full color charts and get your
Video Walkthroughs at himareddy.com/gann2bonus

Figure 4.24.E V

Created with ©TradeStation Technologies, Inc. All rights reserved.

On Aug 1, 2018, I published a video update that included coverage of the Verizon (V) stock chart. It displayed two PRICE Top Poke BUY patterns. [9]

Figure 4.24.E shows Verizon posting a high at 136.69 on Jun 20, 2018. Price returned to that high for a PRICE Top Poke BUY on Jul 30, 2018, holding at 135.31.

Then, the next move higher produced similar price action. Price pulled back to 142.54 on Sep 6, 2018 to "poke" the 143.14 old high (Jul 27, 2018).

Gann Selling Point #1: "SELL at OLD TOPS or OLD BOTTOMS..."

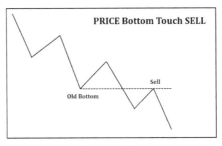

Figure 4.25.A

Holding at an old bottom level is a good indication of the weakness of the market. This is called PRICE Bottom Touch SELL.

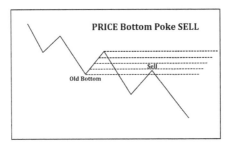

Figure 4.25.B

Finally, PRICE Bottom Poke SELL illustrates when the market rallies just above the old bottoms. Depending on how far up the market goes and where it trades from there, this may indicate strength. However, if the market turns back below the old bottom soon after poking above it (less than 25%), this can provide easy-to-find, low-risk opportunities to enter short in a downtrend.

In each of these scenarios, there needs to be a uniform approach regarding the validation or violation of any old bottom as a resistance level.

Based on my observation of Gann's two bar rules (explored later on in this book), the general rule is to **wait for two session closes above a particular resistance level before disregarding that level as**

resistance going forward. This falls in line with the test failure concept introduced in this chapter as well.

Figure 4.26, CLWR, Daily, as of Jun 3, 2011
Created with ©TradeStation Technologies, Inc. All rights reserved.

Figure 4.26 shows Clearwire Corporation stock. The underlying chart was examined in the first edition of this book. Now, I've applied the Touch and Poke analysis. The stock initiated a downtrend off the $8.82 high (Sep 30, 2010) with the break below $5.99 (Jul 20, 2010 low). The market fell to $4.63 (December 21, 2010 low) before rallying back towards the old bottom at $5.99.

This created a PRICE Bottom Touch Sell setup, as there was just a 1 cent test of the old low on Jan 6, 2011, posting a high at $6.00 (shown on chart).

The market then consolidated for a few months, but the entire range was capped by the $5.99 old bottom which provided several short opportunities:

The first was a PRICE Bottom Touch SELL on Feb 4th ($6.00 again). And the next was a PRICE Bottom Poke SELL on Apr 7th that capped at $6.11 (shown on chart).

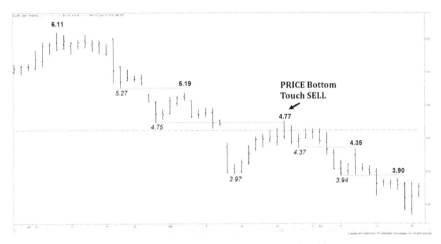

Figure 4.27, CLWR, Daily, as of Jun 21, 2011
Created with ©TradeStation Technologies, Inc. All rights reserved.

Figure 4.27 focuses on the price action following the $6.11 high. The market then declined to $3.97 (May 13, 2011 low) over three sections. The subsequent rally marked a PRICE Bottom Touch SELL at $4.77 (May 24, 2011). This tested the most recent old bottom at $4.75 (Apr 28, 2011) as well as the $4.63 swing low on the first CLWR chart (represented by the dashed line).

As you can see, selling old bottoms is effective on the day-to-day swings within the greater daily chart swings.

*Download and Print your Companion Guide
with full size and full color charts and get your
Video Walkthroughs at himareddy.com/gann2bonus*

Rapid Moves

Gann Buying Point #9: "BUYING RULES FOR RAPID ADVANCES AT HIGH LEVELS. In the last stages of a Bull Market in a commodity, reactions are small. Buy on 2-day reactions and follow up with STOP LOSS ORDER 1c to 2c under each day's low level. Then when the low of a previous day is broken you will be out. Markets sometimes run 10 to 30 days without breaking low of previous day."

Figure 4.28

The focus of the illustration in Figure 4.28 is on the last sentence from the Buying Point, stating "Markets sometimes run 10 to 30 days without breaking low of previous day."

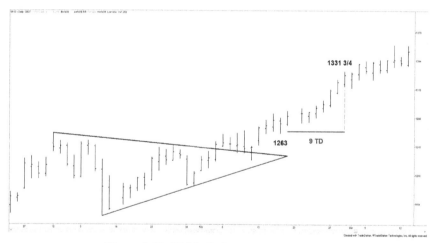

Figure 4.29, SN12, Daily, as of Mar 3, 2012
Created with ©TradeStation Technologies, Inc. All rights reserved.

In Figure 4.29 the daily chart of Soybean Futures (Jul 2012 contract) shows that the market broke higher from consolidation on Feb 13, 2012. A higher low formed at $12.63 (Feb 16) before the market ran up to $13.31 ¾ (Feb 29). This was a run of 9 trading days during which each day's higher low level remained intact.

Gann Selling Point #9: "SELL in the last stages of Bear Market or when there is rapid decline and only 2 days rallies and follow down with stop loss order 1 cent above the high of the previous day. When wheat or any commodity rallies 1 cent or more above the high of the previous day you will be out on stop. Fast declining markets will often run 10 to 30 days without crossing high of the previous day."

Figure 4.30

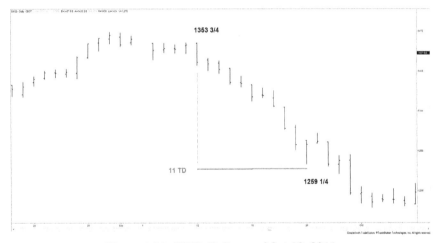

Figure 4.31, SN12, Daily, as of Oct 10, 2011
Created with ©TradeStation Technologies, Inc. All rights reserved.

Just like with the corresponding Buying Point, this example focuses on the last sentence of the Selling Point, which states "Fast declining markets will often run 10 to 30 days without crossing high of the previous day."

Figure 4.31 again shows the Jul 2012 Soybean futures chart. You can see that the market formed a lower high at 1353 ¾ on Sep 12, 2011.

The market plummeted lower to 1259 ¼ (Sep 26, 2011 low). This was a run of eleven trading days during which each day's lower high level remained intact.

Trading Ranges

The market is always trending either up, down or sideways. At first glance, it may seem that Gann's trading points are best applied only to clear uptrends and downtrends. After all, according to him, that's where the greatest profits lie.

However, when the market is trading sideways, it doesn't mean that the market is not tradable. In fact, Gann's basic buying and selling points still appear repeatedly, providing trade opportunities. What changes, however, is the management of the trade and perhaps even the duration from entry to exit.

There are three basic types of sideways price movement.

The first is when range trading occurs at low levels in the market relative to the previous trend. In these situations, **accumulation** is taking place. Figure 4.32 illustrates what happens when large investors build up their long positions in a security before removing a ceiling so that prices can surge higher.

Figure 4.32

Figure 4.32 approximates the types of price movements that occur within a base (range of accumulation). Generally, the upward price moves will occur on greater volume (or open interest, for commodities) than the downward moves. The structures of the upward price moves may even resemble three or four sections up, and the downward moves may resemble corrections.

Clear boundaries generally form on both sides of the range, and they may be straight across as in this figure, or they may slant towards each other (converging boundaries) or away from each other (diverging boundaries).

Another key point to note about accumulation is that the longer the duration of the accumulation phase, the more significant the subsequent breakout. Every subset of sections and corrections within an accumulation phase can be compared to the tightening of a metal spring coil.

Once a boundary is broken and the "tension" is released, the subsequent market action will reflect all the pent-up trading energy that was part of the accumulation process.

The second type of sideways price movement is called **distribution**, during which range trading occurs at high levels relative to the previous trend. Figure 4.33 illustrates large investors decreasing their positions in a security before removing a price floor so that the market can drop lower.

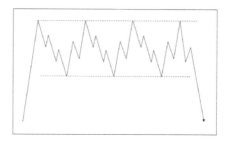

Figure 4.33

It generally takes less time to complete a phase of distribution than a phase of accumulation. This is because the "fear" which is integral to distribution is stronger than the "greed" which fuels accumulation.

The third type of sideways price movement can occur during an uptrend or a downtrend. There are many subsets of these types of sideways movements, which are generally continuation patterns (prior trend eventually resumes). However I'd like to look at a seemingly random consolidation movement.

Figure 4.34 shows a general sideways series of price movements. However, looking closely at the delineated action, you can see that swing highs and swing lows are broken within the overall price action. One could apply the Gann buying and selling points to this scenario to make short-term trades and profit off of the sideways trend.

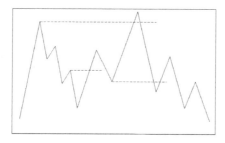

Figure 4.34

Better yet is when the consolidation is not so seemingly random and actually has some clear boundaries to it. Figure 4.35 illustrates consolidation that creates definitive boundaries as it unfolds. The trend preceding the sideways action in this case is up. Therefore, it is likely that the end of consolidation will result in the continuation of the uptrend, illustrated by the breakout at point A.

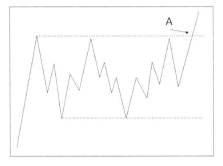

Figure 4.35

In an uptrend, consolidation patterns that imply continuation higher often have a downwards slant. This makes sense because a consolidation pattern is really just a complex correction; therefore it is likely to work against the prior trend. Similarly, in a downtrend, consolidation patterns that imply continuation lower often have an upwards slant.

When attempting to participate in short-term trade opportunities within these boundaries, the best approach is to favor the "slant" of the consolidation, whichever direction that is.

Most importantly, be aware of the direction of the preceding trend at all times. This will keep you better prepared for the eventual breakout.

By using Gann's principles to understand the inner workings of all of these different episodes of sideways market action, you'll be able to capitalize on the short-term movements within these patterns as well as better prepare yourself for breakouts and subsequent trend moves.

"My winning percentage has gone up after working with you. Thank you so much! I am getting more joy from trading now." - Casey C., Georgia

[5] Video Walkthrough: Sep 12, 2018 MNST & CELG

[6] Video Walkthrough: Aug 15, 2018 BIIB & REGN

[7] Video Walkthrough: Dec 13, 2017 GOOGL

[8] Video Walkthrough: Jun 27, 2018 GOOGL

[9] Video Walkthrough: Aug 1, 2018 V

If you would like to view these charts larger and in full color, you can Download and Print your Companion Guide and get your **Video Walkthroughs** at himareddy.com/gann2bonus

5

Application of Gann's Principles

In this chapter, I present how I've made what Gann wrote my own. This practice is crucial to your continued study of Gann's works. You must mold and shape the principles that Gann presents into different but related concepts.

This is critical for two main reasons.

First, Gann does not share his secrets easily, as you've seen if you've attempted to read his books on your own.

Second, we can never emulate exactly how he used the information he presented. We were not there to watch him move through his analysis routines. We do not know (as a fact) how he made his trading decisions.

So, it's in our best interest to look at each tenet he shared from different angles.

Gann's Favorite Numbers

Earlier, we explored eights retracements and projections. I introduced the numbers and ratios that Gann deemed most significant in his study. I shared how Gann prioritized buying and selling patterns. Now, we'll look at the importance of mathematical relationships in the market as per Gann. Some of these relationships translate to types of support or resistance levels.

I will also show how I've taken what Gann wrote and "made it my own". This practice is crucial to your continued study of Gann's works. You must take the elements Gann presents and shape them into concepts you can apply.

100% retracement

Consider a price range with an extreme high and an extreme low. The 100% retracement is the complete overlap of this move. It is a significant level because of human psychology.

Many have debated whether "the market" has a memory, and reacts to past high and low prices because of it. Whether the market has a memory or not is not the issue. What's key is that human beings trade the market, and humans have memories.

It doesn't matter whether you're considering a human being trading alone or in a group. Anyone trading a market can access the historical data on that market. And they can find out what the extreme high and low prices are. It's our perception of "too high" and "too low" that then comes into play.

The 100% retracement signals a full return back to a price level that was "too high" or "too low" in the past. So, the price action that unfolds from that point will depend upon the potency of its market memory.

50% retracement

The 50% concept is one we've already explored in this book. There are several ways that Gann presented the 50% retracement to be of importance. The first was when it was 50% of the range from the extreme high to the extreme low (main half-way point). The significance of this is direct enough.

Another way Gann found 50% to be valuable was when there was a cluster of 50% retracements near the same level. It was also helpful to see a 50% retracement clustered with other types of retracement levels.

What I want to encourage here is taking this out a few steps. **Gann emphasized the 50% level as the most important retracement within the eighths.** We've applied retracements to highs and lows to find support and resistance levels. The actions include a subset of elements. Retracements measure the element of price.

But let's look at the other elements present—time, patterns, and reversal bars.

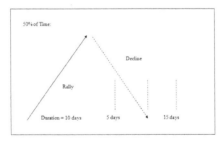

Figure 5.1

Figure 5.1 is an illustration of the concept of looking at 50% of time. Start by looking at the amount of time present within a move upon which you could draw retracements. I've illustrated a low to high move with a duration of 10 days.

As time elapses, we can expect that price may exhibit significant action at the 50% retracement of time based on the previous move. 50% of 10 equals 5. So, we project the 5-day retracement forward and note the likelihood of significant price action at day 10 and day 15.

This relates to a topic which has stumped technical analysts studying time in the past. The markets are not open every single day. And charts do not always account for weekends or holidays by keeping "white space."

So, should we measure time calculations according to calendar days or trading days?

When I first pondered this issue, I noted that this is only an issue on daily or intraday charts.

So, the solution might've been to apply time analysis only to weekly timeframe or higher charts. This would allow me to get a feel for market movement along the X-axis of time.

And this would be a new way of looking at things since as traders we are generally more focused on the Y-axis of price.

I could still return to charts with a time-frame of daily or intraday for time analysis. But I would be better able to compare the observations made using calendar days versus trading days.

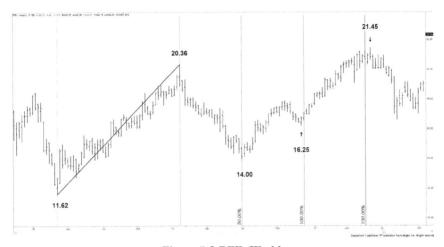

Figure 5.2 PFE, Weekly
Created with ©TradeStation Technologies, Inc. All rights reserved.

Figure 5.2 shows a weekly chart of Pfizer, Inc. The advance from $11.62 (Mar 2, 2009 low) to $20.36 (Jan 20, 2010 high) lasted 47 weeks.

The market reversed lower off $20.36. During the 24th week (50% of the 47-week advance) of the move down, the market posted a low at $14.00 (Jul 1, 2010).

The market continued to follow this time rhythm, showing turning points highlighted by projections of the 50% time retracement.

The $16.25 low (Nov 29, 2010) came in a week before the 100% time projection, and the $21.45 high (May 31, 2011) came in two weeks after the 150% projection.

This application of 50% to time analysis is directly related to the study of cycles in market action.

I will talk about cycles more later in this book. The point of this exercise is to show how Gann's most important mathematical relationships can be studied and applied in ways that extend beyond the examples presented in his works.

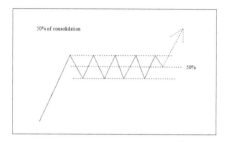

Figure 5.3

Figure 5.3 illustrates the idea of looking at 50% within a consolidation formation.

Distinct boundaries may form as trading continues in a sideways range. Those boundaries may be parallel, converging (triangular), or diverging.

Calculating the price retracements of the range, no matter what style boundary, will yield a 50% value to watch where significant price action may develop.

Figure 5.4 ALU, Weekly
Created with ©TradeStation Technologies, Inc. All rights reserved.

Figure 5.4 shows a weekly chart of Alcatel Lucent. A period of sideways trading occurred after the $18.32 high was posted (Mar 8, 2004), with a lower boundary at $10.44 (Jul 7, 2005 low).

The 50% retracement of the $18.32/$10.44 range is 14.38. This was a level to monitor for significant price action.

On Jul 3, 2007, the market posted a swing high at $14.57. This high was just 19 cents above the 50% retracement level.

Then the market moved lower and eventually broke below the $10.44 boundary.

Figure 5.5 GPBUSD, Weekly
Created with ©TradeStation Technologies, Inc. All rights reserved.

Figure 5.5 shows a weekly chart of GPBUSD. In a video on Jan 17, 2018, I pointed out the 50% retracement levels as shown here. [10]

The 1.4119 level that I marked represented the 50% retracement of a large range weekly bar that formed during the week ending Jun 24, 2016.

If the currency pair were to trade higher through that level, the next marked resistance was at 1.4464, which equaled the 50% retracement of the long term decline from the week ending Jul 18, 2014 through the week ending Oct 7, 2016.

As you can see, this band of resistance levels ended up capping the advance higher off the 1.1739 low.

Download and Print your Companion Guide
with full size and full color charts and get your
Video Walkthroughs at himareddy.com/gann2bonus

Figure 5.6 CTRP, Daily
Created with ©TradeStation Technologies, Inc. All rights reserved.

Figure 5.6 shows a daily chart of CTRP Ctrip.com. In a video on Mar 14, 2018, I pointed out the 50% retracement level as shown here. [11]

The $49.56 price levels equals the 50% retracement of the fall from the $56.46 high (Oct 07, 2017) to the $42.65 low (Dec 11, 2017).

This area ended up providing resistance through Mar 21, 2018, ultimately forming a high at $50.25. From there, futures traded lower through the $42.65 swing low.

Figure 5.7 AUDUSD, Daily
Created with ©TradeStation Technologies, Inc. All rights reserved.

Figure 5.7 shows a daily chart of AUDUSD. I posted a video update on currency pairs at key Gann levels on Aug 8, 2018. [12]

Here, price action was range-bound as a triangle (see converging black trendlines). And, the entire triangle was capped by the 50% retracement, at 0.7493, of the decline from 0.7677 (Jun 06, 2018) to 0.7310 (Jul 02, 2018).

From there, the triangle resolved to the downside (breakdown in price).

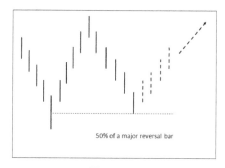

Figure 5.8

Figure 5.8 shows a series of price bars. The first swing low represents a major reversal bar in a market. By "major", I mean an extreme high or an extreme low level. Measuring the 50% retracement of just that one bar will yield a potential key area (in this case, support).

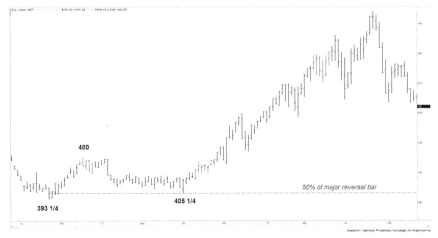

Figure 5.9 CN12
Created with ©TradeStation Technologies, Inc. All rights reserved.

Figure 5.9 shows a weekly chart of Corn futures (Jul 2012 contract). This contract posted its extreme low at $3.93 ¼ (Sep 4, 2009). It rallied to post a high at $4.80 (Nov 16/17, 2009) then edged lower. About ten months after the extreme low was posted, corn futures fell to $4.05 ¼ during the week of Jul 2, 2010. This low held 3 ticks above the 50% value of the extreme pivot low range (bar high $4.16 ¼, bar low $3.93 ¼, 50% at $4.04 ¾). This support held and became the base low for the advance that lasted for the next 14 months.

Figure 5.10 SWKS, Daily
Created with ©TradeStation Technologies, Inc. All rights reserved.

Figure 5.10 shows a daily chart of Skyworks Solutions. In the same Mar 14, 2018 video reviewing Nasdaq 100 stock picks, I pointed out that SWKS had traded precisely up to key resistance. [11]

This level was the 50% retracement, or midpoint, of the entire Nov 6, 2017 range, or price spike.

The midpoint was $115.98, and a high had just formed (relative to the video date) on Mar 12, 2018 at the exact same level.

You can see that a sharp fall in price developed from this lower high, and price trended lower into the end of 2018.

Figure 5.11, DHI

Figure 5.11 shows a daily chart of DHI. This was among the range-bound stocks that I reviewed in a video on Apr 25, 2018. [13] Here, price action was range-bound in that it was shaped by two prior session ranges.

The entire Feb 7, 2018 range provided resistance.

Note that on both Apr 5, 2018 and Aug 21, 2018, price was not able to close above the midpoint of the Feb 7, 2018 range.

Reviewing price support, the price range from Mar 2, 2018 provided support on Apr 2, 2018.

The support range was then violated in line with the dominant down-trend.

Any Level of Eighth Retracement

Even though I've shown many examples focusing on the significance of the 50% retracement, remember that you should study and observe all of Gann's favorite mathematical relationships to see how they allow you to focus in on pressure points in the market where significant time or price action may occur.

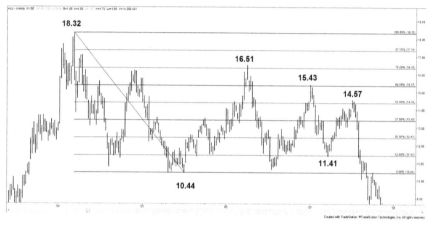

Figure 5.12 ALU, Weekly
Created with ©TradeStation Technologies, Inc. All rights reserved.

Figure 5.12 returns to the same Alcatel Lucent data that's in Figure 5.4, but this time I've applied a full set of eights retracements to the chart.

You can see that the 50% retracement level was not the only one to prove significant in terms of price action.

- The $16.51 high (Apr 5, 2006) tested the 75% retracement at 16.35.
- The $15.43 high (Jan 3, 2007) tested the 62.5% retracement at 15.37.
- The $11.41 low (Mar 23, 2007) tested the 12.5% retracement level at 11.43.

Download and Print your Companion Guide
with full size and full color charts and get your
Video Walkthroughs at himareddy.com/gann2bonus

Trading Gaps

Gaps are open spaces on price charts in which there is no traded price action. These generally occur more often in markets that have trading hours that do not span 24 hours. They are very common in individual stocks.

Therefore it is important that I bring, new in this second edition, a conversation about how to best analyze and trade gaps incorporating Gann's analysis approach.

The 50% retracement has many applications to the study of price action. This goes the same for gaps.

When a market gaps higher, my recommendation is to **locate two key points.**

- The first is the **high of the price bar preceding the gap.**
- The second is the **low of the price bar during which the gap occurred.**

Then, using your charting software's retracement tool, draw a measurement from the first point to the second, noting the 50% level or midpoint of the gap.

This in turn provides you with the middle of the gap, which I have found to be an extremely reliable support across a variety of markets and time frames.

Figure 5.13 NFLX, Daily
Created with ©TradeStation Technologies, Inc. All rights reserved.

Take a look at Figure 5.13 of Netflix. There was a gap higher in Jan 2018 from the $227.79 high (Jan 22, 2018) to the $248.02 low (Jan 23, 2018).

The 50% retracement of the gap, calculated with the method just described, is $237.91. After initially trading higher, shares did return to the gap.

They formed a low at $236.11, after testing the midpoint of the gap for just one trading session. From there, the stock soared higher.

When a market posts a gap to the downside:

- First determine the low of the bar preceding the gap.
- Next, find the high of the bar that created the gap.
- Again, take the retracement tool and connect these two points, noting just the 50% level in the middle.

Sometimes, **gaps are very large relative to the average trading range** of the security analyzed. In these situations, you can usually discern additional support or resistance levels by applying the 25% and 75% retracements.

When the size of a gap is three times or more the average range of that market at that time, then bringing these two retracements can add great analysis value.

It's not often that I discussed the sub elements of the price bar in relationship to candlesticks in this book. But when both of the bars that create a gap have long wicks shadows, then it is to your benefit to also calculate the 50% retracement of the gap based on the closing values of the price bars that created the gap (not just the extreme ends of the shadows).

So when the market gaps higher:

- First locate the close of the bar preceding the gap.
- Then locate the close of the bar during which the gap occurred.
- Then, again using your retracement tool, you would measure from each of these closing prices to determine the 50% midpoint.

This tool can even be used to layer upon the retracement you already drew based on the high and low set up.

When the market gaps lower, again:

- Locate the close of the bar preceding the gap.
- Then locate the close of the price bar during which the gap occurred.
- Then measure the 50% retracement of these two levels.
- You can layer that retracement over the 50% measure from the high of the gap to the low of the gap based on the entire price bar range.

Figure 5.14 CELG, Daily
Created with ©TradeStation Technologies, Inc. All rights reserved.

Take a look at Figure 5.14 of Celgene, CELG.

There was a gap lower in Oct 2017. Both candles that produced the gaps had long lower shadows.

The closing value on the candle before the gap was $119.56 (Oct 25 2017). The closing value on the candle after the gap was $99.99 (Oct 26 2017). The 50% retracement of the gap, calculated with the method just described, is $109.78

Shares did return to the gap. They formed a high at $110.81, testing the midpoint of the gap twice. From there, shares declined.

Traditional technical analysis teaches that the markets don't like gaps. What this means is that gaps are often filled. The challenge to this statement is that there is no time perspective provided.

How can we know when the gap might be filled? This is when it is advisable to **look at the length in time of the move preceding the gap**. We're talking about one singular directional move before the gap took place. Then, project that time out by a factor of 1.

For example, if the duration of a rally before a gap up was 20 days, then be aware that over the following 20 days from the formation of the gaps there is a higher chance that the gap will be filled.

If the gap is not filled during those 20 days, it doesn't mean that it never will be, it just suggests that it is unlikely to happen any time soon, and so you shouldn't count on it.

Gann's Principles Applied to Analytical Tools
Trendlines

One of the most useful books I studied during my CMT exam preparations was *Technical Analysis of the Financial Markets* by John Murphy. I was familiar with many of the basic technical analysis concepts presented in the text before I read it for the exams.

I really appreciated the approach that Murphy used to define and explain those concepts. So, I will reference some of his definitions for technical trading tools.

The first to address is the trendline. Murphy defines trendlines by directional movement.

"An up trendline is a straight line drawn upward to the right along successive reaction lows.

A down trendline is drawn downward to the right along successive rally peaks."

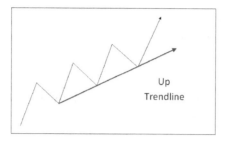

Figure 5.15

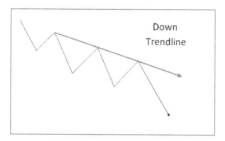

Figure 5.16

Murphy then goes on to say "A tentative up trendline is first drawn under two successively higher lows, but needs a third test to confirm the validity of the trendline."

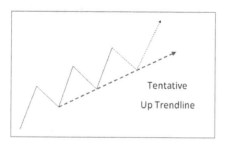

Figure 5.17

I believe that any technical tool that you add to your charts is only of great value if it does one of two things. First, if it helps you trade with the trend. Second, if it helps you become aware of potential areas for trend reversal.

One tenet that Gann repeated is that once the market has tested a level three times, it is more likely that it will break through that level than hold it a fourth time. So if that is the case, what are the limits of the traditional trendline, which contains three connecting points and measures their trend?

I have observed that the trendline will not always provide secure trade entry points all on its own. What it will do, however, is show a trader where the trend *may change,* at least in the short term.

Figure 5.18, ESU11
Created with ©TradeStation Technologies, Inc. All rights reserved.

Figure 5.18 shows a 15-minute chart of E-mini S&P 500 futures (Sep 2011 contract).

- After the market formed a low (Anchor), the subsequent higher low (2nd point) provided the means to draw a "tentative" trendline.
- A subsequent higher low (3rd point) then "confirmed" the trendline as a rising support according to the traditional definition.
- However, the next touch of the line—the fourth attempt—showed price breaking below the trendline.

Even though this example is of a 15-minute time frame, this can occur on any time frame. Let's take a look at another example, where the breakdown occurred awhile after the trendline was confirmed.

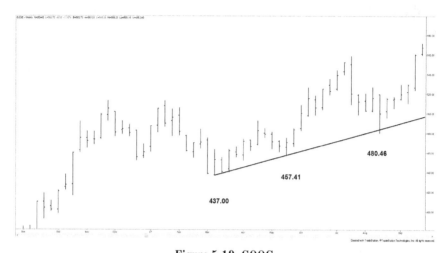

Figure 5.19, GOOG
Created with ©TradeStation Technologies, Inc. All rights reserved.

Figure 5.19 shows a weekly chart of Google, GOOG. After the market formed an anchor low at $437.00 (Mar 5, 2007).

The subsequent higher low at $457.41 (May 15, 2007) provided the means to draw a "tentative" trendline.

A subsequent higher low at $480.46 (Aug 16, 2007) then "confirmed" the trendline as a rising support by the traditional definition. One would then expect that a return to this line would hold as support.

Figure 5.20, GOOG
Created with ©TradeStation Technologies, Inc. All rights reserved.

However, moving forward several months on Figure 5.20, the market rallied to $747.24 (Nov 7, 2007) before turning lower.

The next touch of the trendline—the fourth test—shows that price broke below the trendline. Within a couple of weeks, the former trendline reverted to resistance, as shown with the pivot high that formed at $541.04 (Feb 14, 2008).

A couple of months later, the former trendline became an approximate center axis for a zone of consolidation which ultimately formed a lower swing high at $602.45 (May 2, 2008).

Even though the chart shown is of a weekly time frame, once again this type of price action can and does occur on all time frames. The examples presented are intended to guide you to make practical use of trendlines in your analysis, not to just follow them blindly.

Another way to use trendlines towards greater analytical prowess is to revisit the key elements which compose a trendline.

By the traditional definition, two highs (or lows) create a tentative trendline, and a third high (or low) confirms the trendline.

However, what would happen if we used the *range* of the high or low to create a pair of trendlines?

Figure 5.21, GOOG
Created with ©TradeStation Technologies, Inc. All rights reserved.

Figure 5.21 shows a daily chart of Google, GOOG. A rising trendline originating from the $433.63 low (Jul 1, 2010) connected to the $473.02 low (Jun 24, 2011), and was confirmed on Oct 4, 2011, posting a low at $480.60.

However, if one had projected a parallel of the tentative trendline from the high of the Jul 1st origination bar (high value is $448.40), the trendline channel would have alerted the trader when the $490.86 low (Aug 19, 2011) came in.

Looking at the upper half of the chart, a declining trendline off the $642.96 peak (Jan 19, 2011) joined the $641.73 high (Jan 21, 2011), and was confirmed by the $631.18 high (Feb 18, 2011).

If a projected parallel of the trendline had been drawn off the low value of the Jan 19 origination high (low value is $629.66), the trader would have been alerted at the formation of the $595.19 swing high near the projected line (Apr 1, 2011).

Oscillators

Many traders and investors who use technical analysis methods to make their buy/sell decisions use indicators derived from price action as part of their trading plans. One category of indicators is that of oscillators. An **oscillator** is a price-derived indicator which "oscillates" (moves back and forth) between 0 and 100.

The Relative Strength Index (RSI) is a commonly used oscillator. In the traditional approach, when the RSI crosses above 70, the security is considered "overbought", indicating that buying power is waning. When the RSI is below 30, the security is considered "oversold", indicating that selling power is losing force.

Although oscillators may be applied to a chart and observed for signals during trending as well as non-trending markets, the key to using oscillators effectively is to use them differently during each of these trend scenarios.

The value of oscillators is in being able to discern extreme areas in a market.

So, when the market is **trending**, the movement of the oscillators can point to the likely continuation or reversal of the trend.

During **non-trending** market times, the oscillators can help point out the best entries and exits for short-term trades within a consolidation range, accumulation phase, or distribution phase.

So, why am I talking about oscillators when Gann never did? Because if oscillators are price-derived, and Gann uncovered clear tradable patterns that occur in price movement, isn't it possible that such patterns can also reveal themselves within the oscillators? Let's take a look and find out.

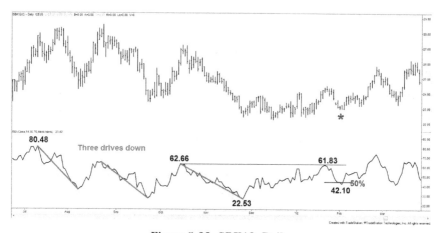

Figure 5.22, SBK12, Daily
Created with ©TradeStation Technologies, Inc. All rights reserved.

Figure 5.22 depicts the May 2012 contract of Sugar No. 11 futures. The RSI made three sections down from the 80.48 value (Jul 12, 2011).

The thin horizontal line drawn out from the 62.66 value (Oct 14, 2011) towards the 61.83 value (Jan 23, 2012) highlights the fact that the rally from the 22.53 low value (Nov 25, 2011) retraced nearly all of the RSI section down from Oct. More significantly, the period of time of the rally from 22.43 to 61.83 "exceeded the last rally before extreme lows were reached."

This movement compares directly to the previously described **Gann Buying Point #5!**

The rest of that Buy signal description says, "If the last rally was 3 or 4 weeks, when the advance from the bottom is more than 3 or 4 weeks, consider the trend has turned up and commodities are a safer buy on a secondary reaction."

This can be directly compared back to the behavior of the RSI in Figure 5.19. The RSI fell from 61.83 to 42.10 (Feb 2, 2012), testing 43.96, the 50% retracement of the 22.43/61.83 section up.

Therefore, the price low marked with an asterisk indicates a buy zone that is reinforced by the Gann signals present within the RSI. I dive deep into this oscillator pattern, and more, in my RSI Power Zones System [14].

Another commonly used oscillator is Williams % R.

As with the RSI, the Williams % R oscillator moves between 0 and 100. When Williams % R is over 80, the security is considered "overbought". When the Williams %R is below 30, the security is considered "over-sold".

One of my coaching students introduced earlier in this book, Elaine C., was a student of Larry Williams before she began her mentorship with me.

The great thing is that we didn't toss what was working for her and start from scratch for the sake of it. Instead, we took the indicators and strategies she learned from Mr. Williams, and we incorporated Gann strategies and more to amplify the power of those strategies.

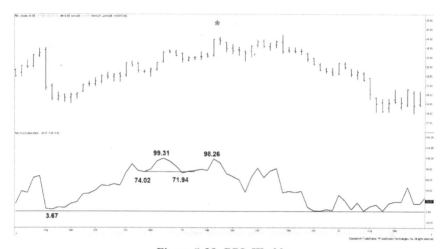

Figure 5.23, PBI, Weekly
Created with ©TradeStation Technologies, Inc. All rights reserved.

Figure 5.23 depicts Pitney Bowe. The Williams % R made three sections up from 3.67 (week of Aug 13, 2010 value) to 99.31 (week of Dec 17, 2010 value).

The thin horizontal line drawn out from the 74.02 value (week of Nov 26, 2010) towards the 71.94 value (week of Jan 7, 2011) highlights the fact that the decline from the 99.31 value broke below the 74.02 value. This move had "broken the bottom of the last reaction, turning trend down."

This movement compares directly to the previously-described **Gann Selling Point #3!**

The earlier part of that selling point description says, "Sell on a *secondary rally* after…". Comparing this description directly back to the behavior of the Williams % R in this example, the secondary rally came in at 98.26 (week of Feb 11, 2011 value).

The price high marked with an asterisk indicates a sell zone marked by the Gann signals present within the Williams % R.

However, it is paramount to remember that PRICE IS KING, and applications of Gann analysis to other price-derived elements (such as oscillators) is only of secondary importance.

In this scenario, the bearish action of the Williams % R would have cautioned longs to tighten their stops, but the oscillator behavior is not meant to be used as a "call to trade action" all on its own.

Where it would come into play is several bars later when price would fail to post higher highs on a closing basis, and the Williams % R action would reinforce a subsequent short position.

The Importance of the Closing Price

After first studying Gann's buying and selling points as delineated in the *Commodities* book, I began to observe the market to practice identifying these signals.

However, I often found that I would look at the overall OHLC bar action and not understand why a certain signal played out the way that it did.

Over time I observed the following—when there was a test of a key support or resistance in the market, but a failure of the subsequent price bars to post a close decisively through that level, this often led to a change in the expected price action.

Take a look at Figure 5.24 depicting weekly price action of Bank of America.

Figure 5.24, BAC, Weekly
Created with ©TradeStation Technologies, Inc. All rights reserved.

Figure 5.25 BAC, Weekly
Created with ©TradeStation Technologies, Inc. All rights reserved.

Figure 5.25 zooms in towards the top of the price action, where a higher high was posted at $18.64 on Oct 14, 2009.

About six months later, the market rallied to test that level during the week of Apr 9, 2010.

The next week saw trading reach as high as $19.86 (Apr 15, 2010), but the week closed at $18.05, a price level below $18.64.

The week following the $19.86 high saw trading reach $18.91, but again the closing price failed to surpass $18.64, this time falling at $17.87. Lower highs and lower lows followed suit.

These probes above $18.64 but failure to sustain a breakthrough on a closing basis once again illustrate the concept of the "test failure".

This particular example is of a **bearish test failure**, since a drop in prices followed.

Moving to a daily chart, Figure 5.26 shows that the market posted a steady decline from the $19.86 peak.

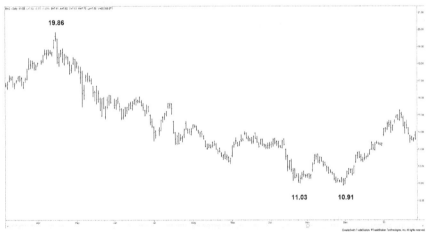

Figure 5.26, BAC, Daily
Created with ©TradeStation Technologies, Inc. All rights reserved.

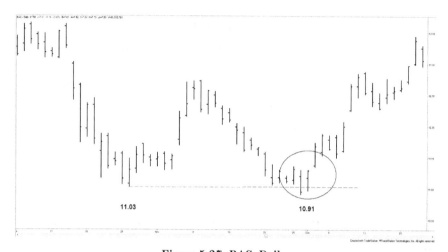

Figure 5.27, BAC, Daily
Created with ©TradeStation Technologies, Inc. All rights reserved.

Using Figure 5.27 to highlight the bottom of the chart, we see that a lower low was posted at $11.03 on Oct 26, 2010. About one month later, the market declined to test that level on Nov 30, 2010.

The OHLC bar reached a low of $10.91 before closing at $10.95, which should have indicated that the downside momentum would continue.

However, the very next bar on Nov 31 posted a close at $11.29, back above the key $11.03 level. Higher highs and higher lows followed suit, changing the trend to up off the Double Bottom pattern.

This illustrates an example of a bullish test failure, since a low was tested and a rise in prices followed. As you can see, there is a two-bar window following the initial level test in which the test failure may form.

However, this is not a signal that is meant to be targeted for market entry. Its prime value is in letting you know when a buying or selling pattern is NOT playing out as expected.

The importance of knowing when a pattern is NOT working is that it allows you exit the trade efficiently, protecting as much profit as possible or minimizing losses.

The methods recommended by Gann as to how to maximize profits and minimize losses will be explained further in Chapter 6.

Recognition of test failures is one way that closing prices can add value to your analysis, but there are also others.

As explained in the first chapter of this book, using simple OHLC charts is the best format to help you start your study of Gann's trading methods, since they show patterns relatively clearly.

However, what happens when you are looking at an OHLC chart of a security, whether it's a 5-minute chart or a daily chart, and you find yourself struggling to see the sections that the market has formed, and where the true high and low points exist?

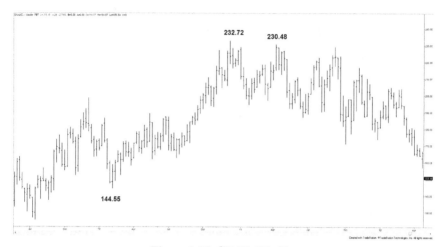

Figure 5.28, $XAU, Weekly
Created with ©TradeStation Technologies, Inc. All rights reserved.

Figure 5.28 of the Gold Cash Index shows the weekly chart peaking at $232.72 (Dec 7, 2010). A lower high formed at $230.48 (Apr 8, 2011) before the index continued lower. The subsequent price action is a bit volatile when comparing the swing sizes to those of the previous advance from $144.55 (Feb 5, 2010).

To get a clear sense of how the uptrend ended, and what exactly is going on within the volatile swings, it would help to look at a simpler version of the chart.

Generally, simplifying a situation involves removing elements of information from it, and the process is no different here.

Instead of studying this chart with the open, high, low, and close of every period (week) shown, convert the image to a line chart. This allows you to focus on one aspect of each trading session—the open, the high, the low, or the close.

The close is desired as the input for a line chart because at the end of a trading session, the closing price represents the agreement that the buyers and sellers have reached regarding the value of that entity for that session.

The opening of the next session, in many cases (especially with shorter-term charts), most often is at or near the closing price of the previous session. Viewing a line chart showing close price only will often clear up any confusion about what sections are present.

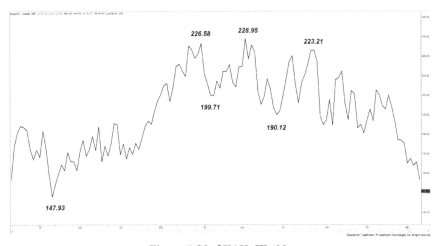

Figure 5.29, $XAU, Weekly
Created with ©TradeStation Technologies, Inc. All rights reserved.

Figure 5.29 shows the close-only version of the Gold Cash Index chart. The high and low points are now labeled in italics because they are indicating the closing highs and closing lows of their relevant time periods. The italics differentiate these values from the actual highs and lows reached, as seen on Figure 5.28.

Based on the line chart, the highest close for the index during the time observed was at $228.95 (Apr 8, 2011). The market made three sections lower to reach $190.12 (Jun 17, 2011 close), breaking below the higher low at $199.71 (Jan 28, 2011 close). The index then corrected higher in two moves, reaching $223.21 (Sep 9, 2011 close).

The weakness from this area occurred in predominantly two-section structures. All of this was easily derived by simply converting an OHLC chart to a line chart based on closing price values.

The importance of the closing price is not only in seeing sections more clearly, but in providing additional "anchor points" for drawing retracements such as Gann eighths.

If the low price of a swing low and the high price of a swing high are good "anchors" for retracements, then calculating retracements of the closing price of a swing low and the closing price of a swing high can help focus in the **true range of market action.**

The lowest low at which a market closed and the highest high at which a market closed over a given period of time shows the true area where supply and demand resided.

Again, this is because the **closing price of any period is where the buyers and sellers agreed on the value of the security**. Drawing retracements from the lowest close to the highest close, therefore, allows you as a trader to focus on the "bulk" of the action.

Figure 5.30 uses the same Gold Cash Index data as the previous figures, but I've added more information to the chart by showing trading from the swing low preceding the full advance up to the Dec 2010 high.

Figure 5.30, $XAU, Weekly
Created with ©TradeStation Technologies, Inc. All rights reserved.

The $70.86 close (Oct 24, 2008) marks the low anchor for the eighths retracements. The $228.95 close marks the high anchor.

Drawing the retracements off of the extreme close levels is capturing the bulk of the move, and keeps you as a trader focused on the zones of support and resistance present.

Too often, we get caught up in a need for a market to rally or decline precisely to retracements we have drawn out, but we hardly ever think about what goes into choosing the anchors for those retracements.

The most obvious benefit of drawing retracements anchored on closing levels is seen with the price action at point (A). That high was posted on Sep 8, 2011, and reached $228.98, only pushing 3 cents above the resistance at 228.95, a sign of the validity of that 228.95 as a resistance level.

"I started working with Hima in January 2020. Because of the plan that she and I discussed during my first 1on1 mentorship session, I was stopped out of long stock positions ahead of the February market crash." - Tim B., Minnesota

[10] Video Walkthrough: Jan 17, 2018 GPBUSD

[11] Video Walkthrough: Mar 14, 2018 CTRP

[12] Video Walkthrough: Aug 8, 2018 AUDUSD

[13] Video Walkthrough: Apr 25, 2018 DHI

[14] Find out more about RSI Power Zones at himareddy.com/myrsi as that is beyond the scope of the work covered here :)

Download and Print your Companion Guide with full size and full color charts and get your Video Walkthroughs at himareddy.com/ gann2bonus

6

Trade and Capital Management

The loss of capital is the number one reason why traders/investors stop participating in the market. Therefore, the importance of preservation of one's capital is of utmost importance. Gann presented capital management rules both directly and indirectly throughout his works. I will boil down the basics of what he presented to get you started on the right foot towards Gann's money management style.

Let's return to the phases of a trade's lifespan as presented earlier in Chapter 4, "Trading the Market":

1. Trend Assessment
2. Signal Observation
3. Risk Assessment
4. Placement of Orders
5. Trade Initiation
6. Management of Trade
7. Trade Exit
8. Review

These phases form a continuous loop. We've covered Trend Assessment and Signal Observation. Now we will explore the remaining phases.

Risk Assessment

In this third phase of a trade, the trader looks at the amount of working capital in the account to construct his trade to manage potential risk. No matter how large or small the amount of capital, Gann's basic tenets, expressed in more than one of his books, provide ways to manage the capital as each trade opportunity arises.

Gann Rule (Affirmative) #1: Divide your capital into 10 equal parts and always risk less than one-tenth of your capital on any one trade.

Now, anyone with trade experience reading the statement above will likely find a trade risking anything close to 10% of one's capital to be too high relative to the account size. I agree with this notion, and I have yet to meet a successful trader who in fact risks 10% of capital on ONE trade.

The main point to glean from the rule is stated as follows: According to the situation described, if the first trade becomes a loss, then the trader would have to be wrong the next nine times in a row to blow out his account. Gann shared that this is extremely unlikely based on the buying and selling tenets that he presented.

Therefore what's important to understand here is that the **less you risk on any one trade, the greater chance you have of preserving your capital in the long haul**. It is up to the individual trader to define the risk per trade, as a percentage or fixed dollar amount, within the confines of the 10%.

- Based on a starting account size of $10,000, the capital would divide into ten equal parts of $1,000 each.

- For the case study, I will employ a 2% maximum risk per trade. For a $10,000 account, that would be $200.

If the first trade is a winner, the account size will obviously increase, however your risk per trade should *not* increase at the point. **The time to adjust the maximum risk capital is once the account has doubled in size.** This means that funds are not to be withdrawn after one or many winning trades. The goal is not to make profits on an unchanging capital amount and then to remove the profits from the account in a piecemeal fashion.

Gann Rule (Affirmative) #11: Accumulate a surplus. After you have made a series of successful trades, put some money into a surplus account to be used as an emergency fund.

The goal as per Gann's money management advice is to make your initial capital work for you.

- When the account doubles to $20,000, remove $5,000 (half the profits) from the account to put into an emergency (or savings) fund.
- Leave the remaining $5,000 (other half of profits) in the trading account. You will now have a total of $15,000 in the trading account.

- Continuing with the 2% risk maximum per trade, the new maximum risk amount per trade would be $300.

On the other hand, if your account is not profitable (losing more capital than you are making), the time to adjust your risk management is when you suffer 3 losses in a row. You would make the adjustments based on your remaining capital.

Gann Rule (Affirmative) #3: Always trade lot sizes and amounts of risk that fit within the limits of your capital.

- Given the guidelines based on a $10,000 account, the minimum capital remaining after three losses in a row would be $9,400, the difference of the initial account balance and the $600 ($200 x 3) lost on the trades.
- So, if you have three losses in a row, risk only 2% of the *remaining* capital.

- Using the $9,400 minimum as a model, the new maximum risk per trade would equal $188.

Now, if the account continues to lose, and at some point suffers three losses once again, you would again take steps to decrease your initial risk.

- Based on the $9,400 new account size, the minimum capital remaining after another three losses in a row would be $8,836, the difference of the initial account balance and the $562 ($188 x 3) lost on the trades.

If three losses occur in a row again, risk only 2% of the remaining minimum capital.

- Using the $8,836 minimum as per our case study, the new maximum risk per trade would equal $176.72.

Gann talks about the trading unit as the number of units (shares, contracts, and so on) of a security involved in one trade. For beginning money management, that does not need to be addressed separately, because the trading unit or "lot size" will directly relate to the rules stated previously. Therefore, if rows of losses occur as described, the number of units traded will decrease in line with the decrease in line with the decrease in the maximum risk per trade.

Gann Rule (Affirmative) #8: Distribute risk equally among traded markets. Only risk up to 10 percent of your capital in any one market.

As you trade a market, and get filled on a position, you may encounter more opportunities to trade the prevailing trend. However, your total risk in any market, no matter how many opportunities to add on arise, should always total less than 10 percent of your capital.

If you see a valid trade signal in another market while you are active in one, you may invest in that second market as well.

The key is to not put all of your eggs in one basket. Keeping your trades diversified and low-risk will make capital preservation that much easier to maintain.

Placement of Orders

Gann Rule (Affirmative) #14: Only enter and exit the market on definite signals with emotions in check.

When I was first learning to day trade, I found it difficult to set up my trades. I would see the pattern, but the three components of the strategy—the entry, the objective, and the protective stop—would not easily pop into my head.

So, my father suggested the following: "When you see a clear pattern that tells you to buy or sell the market you are observing, first ask yourself—'Where would I put the stop?' If you do that, the rest of the trade will fall into place."

I implemented this way of thinking early on and I have always done so since. I'm at the point where I can't even imagine placing a trade without FIRST calculating where the protective stop would need to be.

Gann Rule (Affirmative) #2: Use stop loss orders. Always protect a trade when you make (on commodities) it with a stop loss order 1 to 3 cents (up to 5 cents) away. For cotton, 20 to 40 points (up to 60 points) away. For stocks, 3 to 5 points away.

Although the cents and points presented in this Gann Rule were derived from the way that markets moved during his time, they are still useful guides.

Ultimately, place your stop so that you are risking less than your predetermined amount of capital (2% is the example used) on any one trade.

Gann Rule (Affirmative) #16: Once you've placed a stop loss order, always keep it, and only move it in the direction which minimizes risk/protects profits.

Since I placed my first paper trade, I have determined the price level to place the protective stop loss order on a position. I did this whether I was scalping or trend trading and whether I was buying or selling. This is because Gann's works, the base of my trading education, always focus on the placement of the protective stop, not the determination of the objective.

Along with the very rules shared in the Chapter 4 of this book, for example, Gann added in reminders about how to manage trades.

Included in the description for the listed **Gann Buying Point #8**, he wrote, "Always use STOP LOSS ORDERS for protection in case the market reverses. REMEMBER YOU CAN'T BE RIGHT ALL THE TIME. The STOP LOSS ORDER gets you out if you are wrong. Try to take small losses and large profits. That is the way to keep ahead of the market."

The value of everything that Gann had to say about protecting your trades can not be overstated.

To determine the placement of the protective stop loss order, there are a few options as were described in the Buying and Selling Points.

- Above swing highs/Below swing lows
- Above price bar highs/Below price bar lows

Different ways to assess the stop also exist.

A **money stop** is a stop placed simply based on an allotted risk amount. For example, based on the $10,000 starting capital model, a money stop placed on a long position would not necessarily relate to any actual market movement. It would only directly relate to the maximum loss per trade of $200 based on an estimated entry price.

A **logical stop**, however, takes into account the price action surrounding the entry point. I prefer the use of logical stops, because if they are triggered, they often are clearly telling you that your position in the market was wrong in relation to the trend.

 This breakthrough greatly helped Victor N., my coaching student on the West Coast. He felt compelled to rush into futures market trades, since he did his trading in the early morning hours before heading to work, as many traders do.

When we worked on identifying the placement of the logical stop BEFORE even entering the trade, it really helped Victor stop overtrading.

And, as I often reminded Victor and continue to remind my current coaching students, being stopped out of a trade on a LOGICAL stop is paying for a lesson from the market, on a mistake you may have made and become empowered to not make again. A money stop does NOT provide that same lesson, which can be so, so valuable.

It's important to remember that when using logical stops you must only take action on a trade if the placement of the logical stop still fits within your maximum risk parameters.

There is *no trade worth taking* if it breaks your money management rules. It will be impossible to consistently preserve your capital if you make exceptions to your money management rules.

Per the capital management guidelines explored earlier, traders often come to think of the maximum risk per trade as a goal to reach. Whether they decide that they should risk a maximum of 1%, 2% or 5% per trade, they sometimes seek it out—even when risking that much is not necessary to be able to take advantage of the trade setup.

Instead, traders should look to minimize risk for maximum rewards.

For example, situations may arise where a logical stop fits your maximum risk parameters, and even leaves room for you to increase your lot size within those parameters. In these situations, do not attempt to increase your lot size simply because you have room to do so.

Take the lowest risk trades that fit your trading plan/patterns/ parameters. That is where you will reap the greatest reward.

The real key to placing useful stops is to study the market or markets you trade and observe the following: When the market rallied to prior bottoms while in a downtrend and then resumed lower, by how much (if at all) did the market move above that old bottom?

Similarly, when the market corrected to former tops while in an uptrend and then resumed higher, by how much (if at all) did that market move below that old top?

Knowing this will help you know how much your tickers tests key levels and will allow you to place the most effective protective stop orders.

For example, when trading E-mini S&P 500 Futures on an intra-day basis, I use margins of at least two tick movements to be the starting point for my protective stop placement. Why two ticks or more? I have noticed that very often when there is a false break of a high or low, or a "failure", it is most often only by one tick before the prior trend resumes. Therefore, giving the trade some breathing room prevents some of the situations in which false alarms of direction change trigger stops.

Also, by allowing a failure to play out and still be in the trade, I have time to exit at or near breakeven and reassess the situation.

- If the market is entering a consolidation phase, it will become evident sooner rather than later.
- If the market *did* change trend, I've minimized my loss on re-alization of the change of scenario.
- However, if the market does resume the trend and my trade *would have* been profitable, I can re-enter on a clear signal, as opposed to staying in the trade because of hope.

As Gann wrote, "Trading on hope or fear will never help you to make a success."

Trade Initiation

Gann Rule (Affirmative) #9: Let the market show you at what price to enter a buy or a sell.

Where to enter a market once a signal has been recognized and a stop level assessed ultimately relates to capital preservation, just like everything else in trade management.

However, in the original version of Rule #9, Gann advised to sell at market. Perhaps he meant that literally, as in only use **market orders**. But I believe that what he really meant was that you should pay attention to what the market is telling you about where to enter after a clear pattern forms.

I believe this is because of the way prices fluctuate. They expand and contract directly in line with traders' emotions, which are connected to a multitude of sources, including fundamentals.

Therefore, fixating on a certain price target to enter the market long or short is not going to help you make as much money as being focused on where on the price scale the pattern is occurring and adjusting your entrance plan accordingly.

Management of Trade

Gann Rule (Affirmative) #6: Only enter the market and stay in a trade so long as you are sure of the market indications according to your rules.

Gann Rule (Affirmative) #23: Only change your position in the market with a good reason. When you make a trade, let it be for some good reason or according to some definite rule; then stay in the trade until you have a definite indication of a change in trend.

Sometimes when you read what Gann advises it will sound like a broken record. This is because he wants to drill concepts into your head. These two rules exemplify that.

However, once you have entered a trade, you may decide to add more contracts or shares to your position as the market moves favorably. This is called "pyramiding."

Gann Rule (Affirmative) #21: Select the commodities that show strong uptrend to pyramid on the buying side and the ones that show definite downtrend to sell short.

Gann Rule (Affirmative) #13: Only pyramid on trades that are showing profit. This is how you can make the most profits on sustained moves.

Gann Rule (Affirmative) #20: Pyramid at the right time. On a long position, wait until the security is very active and has crossed Resistance Levels before buying more. On a short position, wait until the security has broken out of the zone of distribution before selling more.

In Chapter 7, "Bringing It All Together", I share an example of a trade that Gann walked through in his *Commodities* book, and it will clearly illustrate how he advised to pyramid.

Now, whether you pyramid on a trade or not, if the trade is moving favorably, you will want to protect your accumulated profits.

Gann Rule (Affirmative) #4: Always protect your accumulated profit. On a long position, raise your stop loss order once your profit equals your initial risk. On a short position, lower your stop loss order once your profit equals your initial risk.

Rule #4 couldn't be clearer. To use it in an example—if you bought 100 shares of stock at a price of $5.00 with a protective stop order at $4.00, your maximum risk of loss is $100 (100 x $1.00).

If the market moves favorably and advances to $6.00, you would have a "paper" profit of $100 and should therefore raise your protective stop to the original $5.00 entry point at the minimum.

If you want to cover the cost of commissions, or lock in some profit, you could raise the stop loss even higher. But the **key is to eliminate the chance of loss as soon as the market presents the opportunity to do so.** Again, this will make capital preservation that much easier to achieve.

Once a stop has moved to breakeven, how do you manage it from there, assuming the market is continuing favorably (you're making money on the trade)? One option is to use **retracements**.

Yes, retracements. They don't have to be limited to use just for entering and exiting trades based on major patterns. They can also be used to manage a trade while it's live. Retracements can provide clear levels for placement of initial protective stop loss orders as well as trailing stops.

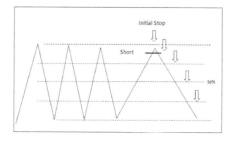

Figure 6.1

Figure 6.1 illustrates a wide-range band of trading with distinct upper and lower boundaries. A short trade initiated near the upper resistance, and the market reversed lower to hold the range as shown.

Instead of focusing on the one or two bar highs within the consolidation pattern for trailing stops, drawing a fourths retracement (breaking down the range into four equal parts) creates new levels to use for adjusting trail stops.

- If the market were to reach the first retracement level, the stop would lower to breakeven.
- If the halfway point (two fourths) was met, the stop would lower to just above the previously met one fourth retracement.
- If the three fourths level were met, in terms of open profit, the stop would move to just above the halfway point.

This provides a clear-cut way to trail stops as opposed to the "traditional" Gann method of two bar highs or lower swings. Basically don't be afraid to take concepts and apply them to different areas of the trade's lifespan.

Another way to manage a trade that is going favorably is to move the protective stop order along bar highs or lows.

Gann talks about runaway trends with great importance, emphasizing that they are the moves in which most great traders' profit is made.

When the market picks up momentum in an uptrend, each session tends to open higher within the range of the preceding bar and very rarely even touches the low of the previous bar.

If a correction appears and extends over the period of two bars or more, it may break the low of one previous bar before the uptrend resumes.

This type of move often affects inexperienced traders the most, as they find the one-bar break to be a sign of trend change and exit their longs, or worse, go short.

The runaway move instead continues higher after the correction that only took out the low of the one most recent bar.

Figure 6.2 illustrates this price action.

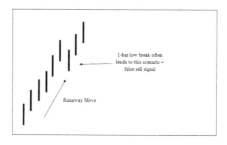

Figure 6.2

Ultimately, the runaway move will cap out for a high or consolidation, but how does one maximize the profit on the long position before this happens? **By watching for the break of the two bars preceding the current one.** When the market makes a correction taking out the two previously-established bars lows, it becomes the first warning of impending trend change. That is the time to tighten stops, or to exit the next attempt at the move higher. Figure 6.3 illustrates the described price action.

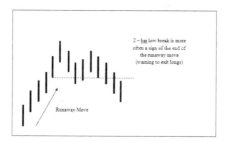

Figure 6.3

Even using the two-bar rule itself for stop placement is reasonable, and I have implemented that as a trailing stop methodology in runaway moves, even down to a 1-minute chart.

The key to obtaining trading success with this information is to get a sense of how each particular market moves.

Take a look at Figure 6.4 illustrating Soybean futures (Jul 2012 contract).

Figure 6.4, SN12, Daily, as of May 1, 2012
Created with ©TradeStation Technologies, Inc. All rights reserved.

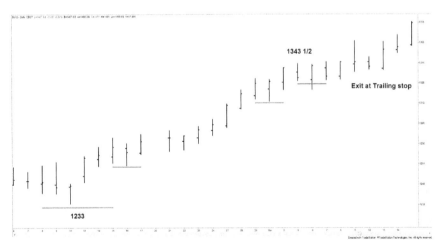

Figure 6.5, SN12, Daily, as of Mar 14, 2012
Created with ©TradeStation Technologies, Inc. All rights reserved.

Figure 6.5 zooms in on the up move from $12.33 (Feb 10, 2012 low) to $13.43 ½ (Mar 5, 2012 high). Placing a 3-cent trailing stop based on one-bar lows would have exited longs at $13.27 ¼, on the break of the $13.30 ¼ low (Mar 5, 2012).

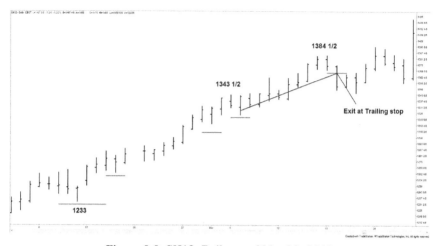

Figure 6.6, SN12, Daily, as of Mar 30, 2012
Created with ©TradeStation Technologies, Inc. All rights reserved.

However, applying a two-bar trailing stop method, Figure 6.6 shows that any long position would have been held longer. The minor correction from $13.43 ½ saw one bar post a lower high and lower low before the uptrend resumed.

Because that second bar had a lower high indicating only a reaction, the trailing stop stayed in position, at $13.20 (3 cents below the low of the bar preceding the 1343 ½ price bar).

However, later on when the market reached $13.83 ¾ on Mar 16, the next day's bar posted a *higher* high at $13.84 ½ as well as a lower low, indicating a reversal. This then made the Mar 16 and Mar 17 bars the reference for the trailing stop, and the stop was moved up to $13.66 ½ (3 cents below the low of the $13.84 ½ price bar).

On Mar 20, the market continued lower and the trailing stop was triggered. The diagonal blue line shows the additional profit captured by using a two-bar trailing stop method as opposed to a one bar trailing stop method.

Notice that I did not talk about where a long may have been entered. That is because I want to keep your focus on the movement of the trailing stops.

It doesn't matter where a long may have been entered after the $12.33 low was posted—what's important is that you see how the way you manage the trade has a direct effect on how much profit you can pull from it.

Overall, your management of a trade should adjust to the market's current character:

In a **sideways** market range, take most of your profits (more than half) at the first objective. Do not hope for a breakout; instead let the market show that it is breaking out of the sideways range.

In a **creeping** (slow moving) market, you can trail stops according to each higher high for longs or lower low for shorts. Or, you can utilize the "auto stop" features of your trading software to help lock in most of the profit (one half to two thirds) of the current potential profit for the move.

In the situations of a **slow** moving market, you should only be giving back a small portion of your net profits if the trailing stop is triggered.

In a **runaway** or **steep** market, the price bar lows/highs on the selected time frame can be used to keep you with the trend. **Remember the two-bar rule.** This will keep you in for the majority of the move.

Figure 6.7, GILD, Daily
Created with ©TradeStation Technologies, Inc. All rights reserved.

I discussed the GILD chart in a video on Nasdaq Stocks on Mar 14, 2018. [15]

I expected higher prices. I was wrong. BUT the important point is here is that **while I had the wrong idea about where the market would go, I had the exact right idea about how to protect any long position**. I pointed out the 2-bar higher low at $80.42 from Mar 12, 2018.

You can see how price broke below that level, and within two sessions (two closing breaks below) it was clear that the up move I was counting on was no longer in play. In this case, price happened to deteriorate and provide a very tradeable downtrend into May.

This brings up the point that when risk/reward parameters allow it, a protective trailing stop can also work well as a trigger for a new position in the opposite market direction to the initial trade.

Figure 6.8 TXN, Daily

In the same Mar 14, 2018 Nasdaq video [15], I reviewed the TXN chart. Again, I expected higher prices within the context of a rising channel.

And again, I was wrong. BUT again the important point is here is that while I had the wrong idea about where the market would go, I had the exact right idea about how to protect any long position. I pointed out the 2-bar higher low at $109.33 from Mar 09, 2018.

You can see how price broke below that level, and along with the exit out of the channel, there was clear evidence that the trend might be changing, or at least pausing. The stock ultimately declined to return to the 96.99 low.

Figure 6.9, AAPL, Daily

Here's one more look at the 2-bar trailing stop approach, this time in combination with trading patterns you learned in Chapter 4. Here's the daily chart of AAPL which I reviewed in a video analyzing Dow Stocks on Jun 20, 2018. [16]

There was an apparent PRICE Top Touch BUY Pattern on Jun 19, 2018 with the formation of the $183.45 low near the $183.50 old high (Mar 13, 2018).

However, that signal evolved into PRICE Top Poke BUY with the formation of the low on $180.73 (Jun 25, 2018). By monitoring 2-bar highs, the latest being at $189.22 (Jun 18, 2018), you would have been prepared for this development.

Download and Print your Companion Guide
with full size and full color charts and get your
Video Walkthroughs at himareddy.com/gann2bonus

Trade Exit

Gann Rule (Affirmative) #10: Only close your trade with a good reason. Follow up with a stop loss order to protect your profits.

Gann Rule (Affirmative) #28: Focus on getting in the market according to your rules and out of the market according to your rules.

The same Buying and Selling patterns, among other tools, that you use to enter the market are the same tools that you can use to exit the market.

Gann Rule (Affirmative) #22: If you have a position on and the market starts to move against it, get out at the market, take your loss, and wait for another opportunity. Or, rely on your stop order to minimize your losses.

Ultimately, there are five ways to exit a trade that respect the rules.

1. An adjusted protective stop is triggered after the market has moved favorably, exiting the trade at breakeven (no loss, no profit).
2. A trailing stop is triggered, locking in profit.
3. The market reaches a predetermined objective and an exit order is triggered at that price, locking in profit.
4. The market goes against the trade and the original protective stop is triggered, taking a loss.
5. The market goes against the trade and you realize you no longer have indications to stay in, so you exit at market, taking a loss.

Review

Reviewing each trade is extremely important, whether it resulted in a profit or a loss.

The first aspect to review reverts back to Rule #28. Ask yourself if you got in the market according to your rules, and if you got out of the market according to your rules.

If the trade was **profitable**...

Gann Rule (Affirmative) #24: Maintain your lot size and maximum risk amount after a long period of success or a period of profitable trades. (Only increase your lot size and maximum risk amount after you have doubled your capital and added back half to your initial account size, increasing your total tradable capital amount).

If the trade resulted in a **loss**...

Gann Rule (Affirmative) #27: If your lot size contains multiple contracts, reduce the number of contracts traded after the first loss.

Overall..

Gann Rule (Affirmative) #15: Take large profits and small losses.

Did you protect as much profit as reasonably possible, according to your rules? If the trade was a loss, did you minimize the loss, according to your rules?

Once the trade has been reviewed at least once, you can return your focus to the market. Sometimes, when you've exited a trade at the end of a strong move, you may quickly see opportunities form to enter the market in the opposite direction (new trend).

Make sure that if you recognize such a pattern, that you only consider taking it if it fits your predetermined risk/reward parameters.

Similarly, if you were in a trade and exited once the market moved against it and you realized you were on the wrong side of the move, after you have reviewed your trade, you may revisit the chart to see if there's an opportunity to enter in the correct direction.

This does not mean you must take the signal—reflecting time after a trade (especially losing ventures) is very important—but this will be an important learning/reinforcement tool for you that will help train your eyes to assess the trend situation more accurately!

If you do decide to take the trade, remember that it must always fit your predetermined risk/reward parameters.

Every trade that you make will not be a winner. But the goal of trading is not to be perfect. The goal of trading is to make money!

By following these tenets and properly managing your trades from beginning to end, you will obtain the skills necessary to be consistently profitable because you will be functioning within a money management system that is focused on **preserving capital.**

"I got so much value out of my 30 minute consultation with you, Hima. I can't wait to spend the next six months continuing work with you 1on1."
- Victor N., California

[15] Video Walkthrough: Mar 14, 2018 GILD & TXN
[16] Video Walkthrough: Jun 20, 2018 AAPL
Download and Print your Companion Guide with full size and full color charts and get your Video Walkthroughs at himareddy.com/gann2bonus

7

Bringing it All Together

Exploring Gann's Examples

Looking at my own copy of *How to Make Profits Trading in Commodities,*
the first 63 ½ pages are pure text, outlining the trading methods and
rules. The rest of the book, through 412 pages, primarily illustrates
examples of the tenets presented in the earlier chapters. Gann moves
from Wheat to Soybeans through the rest of the commodities giving
specific examples of the rules in action.

In earlier works, like *Truth of the Stock Tape* and *Wall Street Stock Selector,*
Gann did include charts within chapters as he wrote, and simultane-
ously analyzed them. However in the *Commodities* book, the charts corresponding to each explanation are not located right up against the
detailed wording.

Through my years of study, this led me to think that Gann wanted me,
as the reader, to take the words and apply them to the chart action myself, "marking up" my own chart to understand the rules at hand.

In the end, when a trader goes to apply the rules, it is to the chart itself,
so why didn't Gann mark the charts with the comments directly?

I believe it's because he understands the power of practice in learning trading rules, and the simple fusion of the word description and the chart by the reader will be their first step towards understanding what he set out to explain.

The 1940-1941 Soybean Trade

My father took this belief out a step by having me study one particular example of Gann's work over and over and over again—an example of a trade on Soybean futures from the *Commodities* book. The original chart is located in the Appendix of this book (See Appendix D).

One page 134, the relevant section begins as follows:

> "TRADING EXAMPLES—Soy Beans—Aug 20, 1940 to October 16, 1941. See chart in back of book covering one to three-day moves and volume of sales and open interest."

Note the mention of volume of sales and open interest. Gann doesn't refer to these in the trade example, as you'll see, but he obviously believed they were important. As you get a handle on the buying and selling patterns presented in this example, as well as the ones previously explored, adding volume and open interest to your charts will be the next step.

Returning to Gann's writing, he goes on to say:

> "These are example of what could have been done by trading according to the rules. It is not my intention to lead anyone to believe that any average human being would get results of this kind, regardless of how well they understood the rules. The reason they would not buy and sell and make large profits of this kind is the HUMAN ELEMENT, which causes a man to act too often on hope and fear, instead of facing facts and following rules."

Gann is outright telling the reader that no "average" human being is destined to reap these results simply by following rules, because something else will come into play. I understand "The HUMAN ELEMENT" to be any and all emotions which are grounded in hope and/or in fear.

Therefore, I believe that Gann is NOT saying that these results are unattainable—I believe he is saying that a human being who has mastered his reactions to emotions based on hope or fear is the type of person capable of achieving these results.

Moving forward to the actual trade analysis, Gann translates each glance at the chart into one line of text. So, the best way that I found to capitalize (educationally, and therefore monetarily) on this setup was to do the following: after finding the chart that corresponds to the text, I would use a large paper clasp to grasp all of the pages in-between to allow for easy flipping back and forth from the trade descriptions to the actual chart. I have found this to be extremely helpful in making more of Gann's verbal descriptions along with the actual charts.

Back to finding the charts, when reading through verbal descriptions of Gann's trade examples, it was natural to want to correspond to the actual chart while reading. However, instead of direction to the page number within the text, I had to return to a listing of charts that is an extension of the Table of Contents and find the correct chart from there.

For this Soybean example, when I finally found the chart for the first time, I wondered, "Why didn't Gann just refer to the page or chart number to begin with?" One answer is that he may have possibly been unsure how the charts would be numbered until he'd finished writing the book, and he didn't have the interest in going back to the text to mark references in order to aid the reader when searching out charts.

Another answer is that he purposely left out the references, so that the reader would have to actually scan through the listing of charts to find the specific one he needed. In this case, "Chart No. 18—Soy Beans 1940 to 1941".

Returning to the text, the first set of trade actions read:

"1940-August 20-May Soy Beans, LOW 69C. The reason for buying was a triple bottom.

> We start with a capital of $1,000 which will margin 5,000 bushels of Soy Beans at 20c per bushel.

> Bought 5,000 May Soy Beans at 70c, placed stop loss order at 66.

> Risk limited to $200 and commission."

Gann says the pattern was a Triple Bottom. However, flipping to Appendix D, you can see that there is no illustration of a Triple Bottom, only a line drawn just below the 70 horizontal marker. Therefore, it is impossible to know where the exact Triple Bottom points were—unless we could look at a chart with every week or day's price data.

Now, as someone who's reviewed this material many times, I have undoubtedly contacted the Chicago Mercantile Exchange and attempted to retrieve a listing of the daily highs, lows, and closes for the May 1940 Soybean futures contract. On all occasions, I have not heard any follow-up.

After agonizing over my inability to obtain these exact records, I realized something—Gann wrote this book in 1942, most likely presuming that readers would have access to the rough data akin to the chart he drew out, and that it would be sufficient. Who had time to call the exchange for over one year's worth of daily Soybean trading data just to better understand a textbook example?

This is why Gann presents many examples, but shares charts in a basic manner without many details. I believe that he was trying to show that **the true lesson is in following the money management that is applied as buy and sell patterns appear in the examples**. All of the details I used to get hung up on, like having precise historical data, were not crucial to my learning of the lesson at hand.

So, for every line of text relating Gann's commentary on a trade to the actual corresponding chart, I've come to use the following procedure to extract the most knowledge from the trade, with the least amount of frustration. I will explain the procedure using the next line of text in the Soybean example as a model.

Step 1: Read the line of text.

"October 8—Raised STOP LOSS ORDER to 74."

Step 2: Ask yourself, "Why did Gann do this?" Asking this question early on will help make decoding his examples a much easier task.

In this case, you would ask yourself, "why was the stop loss raised?"

Step 3: Immediately glance at the chart.

In this example, you'd see that on October 8, May Soybean futures rallied through 79 cents, and established a new higher base at 76 cents.

Step 4: Mark any observations made in the margin of the text, in a separate file of notes, or both.

For this example, I wrote, "raised stop to below latest bottom" in the margin.

Let's analyze the next line in the same fashion.

Step 1: Read the line of text.

"October 29-Raised STOP LOSS ORDER to 81 ¼. Keeping Stop Loss Orders 1c to 3c under bottoms."

Step 2: Ask, "Why did Gann do this?"

In this example, the answer is pretty straightforward. A higher bottom formed, which is why the stop loss (protective stop order) was raised.

Step 3: Immediately glance at the chart.

The chart shows that a higher low formed at 83 cents.

Step 4: Mark any observations.

Here, I simply drew a line connecting my previous margin comment, "raised stop to below latest bottom," to this example's line of text as well.

By moving through Gann's examples using these four steps, you will extract the most knowledge with the least amount of frustration. You will also hone in directly on the trade management lessons that Gann was trying to convey through these many market examples.

Soybean Trade "Recreated"

Flipping back and forth between the text and chart is one way to associate Gann's description of a trade or market movement to its correlating chart. However, for in-depth study, I wanted to do something more thorough.

I racked my brain for a way to make the chart material more useful to study. I wanted the chart itself to present more information that I could ascertain at a glance. I ultimately attempted to use a spreadsheet to re-create the charts using the given data along with the text descriptions.

By breaking down Gann's text into several key elements to tell the "story" of the trade, I plotted the trade action in the form of a Scatter chart (Microsoft Excel) to create a new form of the commodity chart.

The advantages of going through this process were that (a) it gave me a very clear visual description of Gann's trade actions (whether historical or recommended) and (b) it forced me to really immerse myself in the details of everything that Gann laid out.

Examine Figure 7.1, representing the May, 1941 Soybeans sequence of trades described in the *Commodities* book (page 134).

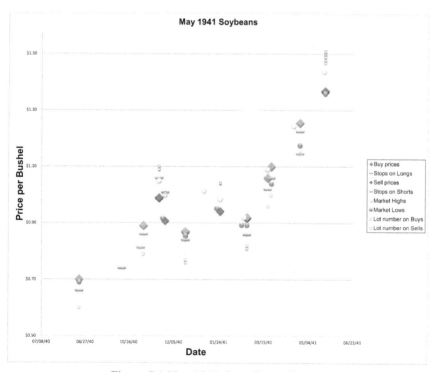

Figure 7.1 May 1941 Gann Beans Trades

Note that I broke down the Soybean trade information into eight components as described in the chart legend. A look at the first set of markers on the far left of the chart will explain how the rest of the markers came about:

In the middle of page 134 of the *Commodities* book, the text says:

> 1940 – August 20—May Soy beans, LOW 69c. The reason for buying was a triple bottom.
>
> We start with a capital of $1,000, which will margin 5,000 bushels of Soy Beans at 20c per bushel.
>
> Bought 5,000 May Soy Beans at 70c, placed stop loss order at 66.
>
> Risk limited to $200 and commission.

Returning to the chart legend, the green solid diamond marker represents the price point (70 cents) and time point (Aug 20, 1940) at which the buy was entered ("Buy Prices").

The purple solid dot marker represents the low (69 cents) made on that same date ("Market Lows").

The solid pink dashed line marker represents the stop loss (protective stop) placed (at 66 cents) on that trade ("Stops on Longs").

And lastly the green square marker represents the number of lots that were traded—buying 5,000 bushels (as explained by Gann) would equal one lot, therefore there is one green box marker ("Lot number on Buys").

Continuing through the text in this manner yields the data necessary for the rest of the chart:

	High made	Low made
08/20/40		$ 0.69
11/18/40	$ 1.0500	
11/22/40		$ 0.9175
11/25/40	$ 1.0000	
12/18/40		$ 0.8550
01/07/41	$ 1.0150	
01/21/41		0.9525
01/25/41	$ 0.9850	
02/18/41		0.8925
02/21/41	$ 0.9200	
02/24/41		0.8925
03/19/41	$ 1.0900	
03/23/41		1.04
04/17/41	$ 1.2450	
04/24/41		1.17625
05/21/41	$ 1.4388	
05/22/41		1.36

Figure 7.2 Highs and Lows of May, 1941 Gann Beans Trade

| Long | | | | Short | | | |
Date	Lot #	Price	Stop if app	Date	Lot #	Price	Stop if app
08/20/40	0.60	$0.7000	$0.6600				
10/08/40			$0.7400				
10/29/40			$0.8125				
11/01/40	0.79	$0.8900	$0.8600				
11/18/40			$0.9900				
				11/18/40	1.09	$0.9900	
				11/18/40	1.10	$0.9900	
				11/18/40	1.09	$0.9900	$1.0600
				11/25/40			$1.0100
				11/25/40	1.01	$0.9075	$1.0100
12/18/40	0.77	$0.8700					
12/18/40	0.76	$0.8700					
12/18/40	0.77	$0.8700	$0.8400				
				01/25/41	1.04	$0.9425	
				01/25/41	1.04	$0.9425	
02/24/41	0.82	$0.9200					
02/24/41	0.81	$0.9200					
02/24/41	0.82	$0.9200	$0.8600				
02/24/41	0.81	$0.9200	$0.8600				
03/19/41	0.96	$1.0600	$1.0200				
03/23/41	1.00	$1.1000	$1.0600				
04/24/41			$1.1463				
04/24/41	1.16	$1.2550	$1.2250				
05/22/41			$1.3688				
				05/22/41	1.47	$1.3688	
				05/22/41	1.48	$1.3688	
				05/22/41	1.49	$1.3688	
				05/22/41	1.50	$1.3688	
				05/22/41	1.51	$1.3688	

Figure 7.3 May, 1941 Gann Beans Trade Complete Data
Table

The only columns that do not contain data directly from the text are the "Lot #" columns. I had to find a way to represent the number of lots bought and sold within the parameters of the X and Y axes.

Therefore I decided to simply offset the Lot number on Buys and Lot number on Sells markers from the Price per Bushel where the trade was made.

For example, revisiting the first set of markers on the far left of the chart, the green square is positioned at the 60 cent level, an offset of 10 cents from the 70 cent buy entry price.

If I had been selling at the 70 cent level, then I would have placed a red square ("Lot Number on Sells" marker) at the 80 cent level, again an off-set of 10 cents, but this time I'm placing the lot marker above the entry price marker (simply for visual ease).

Once this information was in place, I took this new chart out a step fur-ther. I added the lines of text relating to the buying and selling points and the trade management rules in use directly onto the chart using text boxes and arrows.

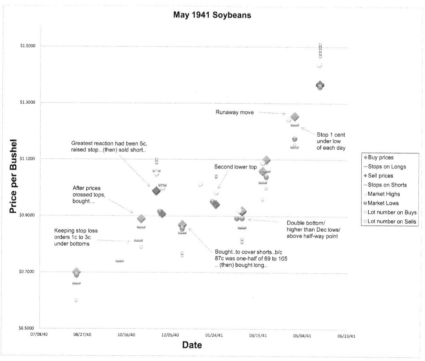

Figure 7.4 May, 1941 Gann Beans Trade "Recreated" with Hima Jedi Twists

Overall, there was educational value for me in creating this chart as well as printing out an annotated copy for regular review. I hope you can see how going through this exercise provided me with a way to piece together many of the concepts explored earlier in this book into a trad-able, usable fashion.

The best way for you to understand Gann's principles is to work through his examples.

Your study doesn't have to be as elaborate as this Soybean example, but it should not be as simple as reading through the example and setting it aside.

Gann teaches through examples, so put your best learning methods to use to get inside his head.

Once you've got a handle on how these patterns and tenets play out in real life examples, you can apply them to your own markets of study and observe as the combinations and sequences of patterns emerge.

Rigid Rules, Flexible Observation

Gann's buying and selling points and trading rules are presented with specific parameters to give you as a trader a framework within which to work. However, one of the keys to successful trading is in being able to adapt to the market situation at hand.

With most trade setups, when you are "with the trend" (in a profitable trade), the trade moves in your direction almost immediately. If it doesn't, that is usually your first clue that you are in a losing trade.

The beauty of Gann's trading methods is that they fit within this framework very nicely. There are clues to watch out for that can tell you relatively quickly if the pattern is going to play out as projected or not.

> *Download and Print your Companion Guide*
> *with full size and full color charts and get your*
> *Video Walkthroughs at himareddy.com/gann2bonus*

Take a look at Figure 7.5 of Corning:

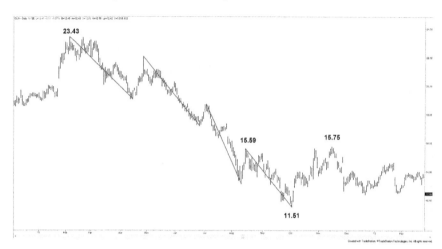

Figure 7.5, GLW, Daily, as of Apr 25, 2012
Created with ©TradeStation Technologies, Inc. All rights reserved.

Figure 7.6 GLW, Daily, As of Dec 23, 2011
Created with ©TradeStation Technologies, Inc. All rights reserved.

The market declined from $23.43 (Feb 4, 2011) to $11.51 (Oct 4, 2011) over the course of 4 sections to the downside.

Zooming in towards $11.51, Figure 7.6 shows that the subsequent rise from the $11.51 bottom first tested the $15.59 resistance level (Aug 15, 2011 high) on Oct 27, 2011, reaching $15.62.

However, the market posted a bearish test failure and returned to $13.71 (Nov 1, 2011 low).

Another move higher took place, and strength retested the $15.59 key resistance one more, reaching $15.75 (Nov 15, 2011 high) however a bearish test failure once again formed. The market then reversed lower into a downtrend.

The test failures were the first clues that this seemingly bullish setup was shaky. There were other clues as well.

Look at the price action from the $11.51 low to the $15.75 high. Notice that it occurred in a series of sections, not one straight move which would have indicated that greed had forcefully overcome fear and bulls were in control.

This illustrates another way to confirm a pattern, which is to look at the structure within the potential pattern formation.

Another aspect of "Rigid Rules, Flexible Observation" comes up in how you perform your chart analysis.

For example, when a tenet is presented, and you have your market that you trade up in the form of a 5 minute chart, **you must be flexible and willing to adapt to observe the market under different conditions.** When sections are not clear on that 5 minute chart, have the flexibility to move down to a 1 minute chart to see the drives more clearly, or up to a 60 minute chart to be sure you're trading within the context of the larger trends.

 When trading live in front of coaching students, especially since it's a day trading focus, this comes into play time and time again. One Group coaching student of mine, Harry V., had not utilized this approach prior to working with me and diving into my foundational education.

After I helped him build his trading plan, we figured out Harry's specific time frames to study based on his personality (he's trigger happy, not gun shy), etc.

When I build out these trading plans, I'm like a dietician. Instead of working with someone's specific genetic story, I help them recognize and sort through their money mindset and money upbringing. Instead of gauging their metabolism, I factor in their current career monetary flow and wealth levels.

Instead of transforming their preexisting beliefs about food or exercise, we transform their views about the markets and trading. This holistic approach helps me to advise my coaching students to boost their trading.

After our analysis, it became clear that Harry had a very clear pathway of his trading time frame, the 3-minute ES futures chart. And he needed to flip back and forth between that 3-minute chart and another longer timeframe, one specific to his trading business goals, so I'm not giving you his prescription here.

This was to help him qualify his trades to improve his odds.

As you study the methods presented in this book within the context of your markets of interest, you will continue to discover the value of knowing the rules, but being flexible as trading situations unfold.

Using more than one time frame can be pivotal to getting the perspective you need to make good decisions.

"**Great introduction to Gann Methodology.** Well done. Reddy discusses the methodology and provides examples, reasoning, history, and other resources that best depict the application of this trading strategy."
- Frank D.

_____

Download and Print your Companion Guide with full size and full color charts and get your Video Walkthroughs at himareddy.com/gann2bonus

_____

8

Beyond Trading Basics

Looking to the Left of the Chart

Gann quoted King Solomon often, and one of the quotes he referred to was, "There is no new thing under the sun." (Ecclesiastes 1:9)

If that's the case, then looking to the left of the chart, at the *history* of a market, has the potential to provide valuable insight into the *future* of that market.

That is what "forecasting" is all about. Now, I know I said that this book will be about Gann's trading methodologies, not his forecasting work.

However, I felt compelled to end this book with a brief foray into the importance of studying past price movement within a specified market. This is because Gann's most advanced (and prized) analysis methods all involve the study and observation of cycles within markets.

The key to being able to understand Gann's more complicated tools begins with your understanding of what a **cycle** actually is. According to Merriam-Webster's online dictionary, the first definition of cycle is, "an interval of time during which a sequence of a recurring succession of events or phenomena is completed."

This definition mentions time, and this is the use of cycles with which most of us are familiar, even outside of trading and the markets.

- We can examine the spans of our lifetimes and see how seasons change four times a year.
- We can examine our 24-hour day and see our sleeping and waking rhythms come into play.
- We can examine the US government and see how actions repeat due to major elections, especially the presidential election, every 4 years.

The list goes on and on.

What will help you grasp Gann's advanced work, as you proceed with your study, is **understanding that cycles apply to every aspect of our universe, and to our trading, not just to time**. In the case of the markets, cycles can be applied to price.

This is why you see old bottoms become new tops (basis of **Gann Selling Point #1**) and old tops become new bottoms (**Gann Buying Point #1**). Definition 2a of "cycle" reinforces this point—"a course of series of events or operations that recur regularly and usually lead back to the starting point".

It may seem at times that prices move haphazardly between zero and infinity, but in fact prices do "recur regularly" and "usually lead back to the starting point," depending on from which point you're measuring.

Definition 2b of "cycle" carries the word that is paramount to using cycles in forecasting—"one complete performance of a vibration, electric oscillation, current alternation, or other periodic process."

The magic word is "**vibration**". Time vibrates. Price vibrates.

Measuring the vibrations of each market you follow is what forecasting is all about. I will present some exercises that you can do to get started on being aware of the vibration or rhythm within the market you trade.

The first step is to look at the OHLC chart of the security on a monthly or weekly basis.

Start as early in the history of the price data as possible, since the more data you can study into the past, the more you can ascertain about the future.

Using Google as an example, the stock was first traded on Aug 19, 2004. I've shared two weekly charts of Google, the first exploring the first "half" of its 12-year life, and the second exploring the second half, as of the 2012 publication of the first edition of this book.

The second step after acquiring data is to mark the significant highs and lows on the chart, especially the **extreme high price** and the **extreme low price**.

Then use a separate daily chart to figure out the precise dates which match the high and low values.

Figure 8.1, GOOG, Weekly, as of Feb 22, 2008
Created with ©TradeStation Technologies, Inc. All rights reserved.

A - $95.96 **extreme low** (Aug 19, 2004)

B - $216.80 high (Feb 2, 2005)

C - $172.57 low (Mar 14, 2005)

D - $317.80 high (Jul 21, 2005)

E - $273.35 low (Aug 22, 2005)

F - $475.11 high (Jan 11, 2006)

G - $331.55 low (Mar 10, 2006)

H - $513.00 high (Nov 22, 2006)

I - $437.00 low (Mar 5, 2007)

J - $558.58 high (Jul 16, 2007)

K - $480.46 low (Aug 16, 2007)

L - $747.24 **extreme high** (Nov 7, 2007)

Figure 8.2, GOOG, Weekly, as of Mar 16, 2012
Created with ©TradeStation Technologies, Inc. All rights reserved.

M - $412.11 low (Mar 17, 2008)
N - $602.45 high (Mar 2, 2008)
O - $247.30 low (Nov 21, 2008)
P - $629.51 high (Jan 4, 2010)
Q - $433.63 low (Jul 1, 2010)
R - $642.92 high (Jan 19, 2011)
S - $473.02 low (Jun 24, 2011)
T - $627.50 high (Jul 26, 2011)
U - $480.60 low (Oct 4, 2011)
V - $670.25 high (Jan 4, 2012)

> *Download and Print your Companion Guide*
> *with full size and full color charts and get your*
> *Video Walkthroughs at himareddy.com/gann2bonus*

Points A through V have been listed in chronological order. However, if you flip to Appendix E of this book, you will see that I have created a list of the same high and low values, but organized them by calendar month, from January through December.

Right off the bat, you should notice that some months contain several instances of significant highs or lows, while other months are devoid of any major market turn during the entire history of trading of this stock.

The month of March shows 5 significant turns. January and July show 4 turns each. August and November show 3 turns each.

So, when trading this market into the future, would you have expected significant changes in trend or market turns to occur during these months? Of course you would have. And a great exercise, as part of your follow up study with this second edition, would be to go back and check that out for yourself! In fact, I teach a systematic way to discovery the relationships between price and time in any given security in my HimaReddy University's inaugural course, Gann 101: Trading Patterns System (himareddy.com/gannuniversity).

You would not trade them blindly, but you would have awareness of the rhythm of this market, the beat to which it has been moving.

Similarly, note that no major trend changes took place in the months of April, May, September, or December. Would you expect turns to occur in those months ahead? Not likely.

Again, this is one of many ways to get to know the rhythm of your market. The more you observe this and the more you study the relationships among highs and lows in the market, the more usable information you will uncover.

Next Steps
Recommended Reading

The first order of business for a serious student of Gann's works would be to read through his original works, as listed in the first chapter of this book.

As mentioned earlier in the book, it is helpful to study Gann's materials in the order in which he published them.

Next, you could explore his specific market courses depending on your area of interest—commodities, stocks, options, etc.

Additionally, you could read the books that Gann read himself. There is actually a list of books that Gann himself stated as recommended reading. It included 81 titles, and the Lambert-Gann Publishing Company has reproduced 21 of them so far.

Gann spent a lifetime studying and reading about the markets. I am not saying that you need to do the same in order to use the valuable knowledge that he shared. My intention is to provide you with a possible path of learning that you can adjust to your desire.

Obtaining Charts

Before you embark on (or return to) studying Gann's original works, I recommend taking time to collect about five security charts. You can save images of the charts in your charting software workspaces or as images from free online sources.

However, the recommended option is to have hard copies (printed on paper) of the charts, whether you are accessing them digitally to start or have hard copies already in a trading newsletter or other chart-based publication.

Make sure that you have one set of copies that you can mark up while keeping a "clean" set of originals.

As for the types of securities to choose for your charts, I believe you will get the most benefit in seeing the universal application of Gann's principles if you **vary your charts**.

For example, you may choose to plot a stock, a commodity future, a currency (FX pair), a fixed income instrument, and a stock index future as your five securities.

You should **vary the time frames** used. The choices are endless, but ideally you want to see different degrees of market movement. For example, perhaps a quarterly chart, a weekly chart, a daily chart, a 60-minute chart, and a 5-minute chart as opposed to a 5-minute chart, a 4-minute chart, a 3-minute chart, a 2-minute chart, and a 1-minute chart.

As computer technology and graphic design continue to advance, the myriad of chart styles available to traders and investors is vast and can be overwhelming. The most basic chart depicts the price action only—open, high, low, close (OHLC)—in the form of bars or candlesticks.

There are Kagi charts which incorporate volume into candlestick charts. There are trading systems out there which color code basic bar charts to extrapolate continuations or changes in trend based on each bar's directional movement. Many of these charts are useful to a variety of students of the market when combined with oscillators and other studies. However, these types of indicator-synthesizing charts are not crucial to understanding Gann's basic tenets. In fact, they may confuse a beginner student.

Therefore I recommend that you **plot the charts as OHLC charts**, as I've done with most of the case studies in this book. Once you've plotted your charts as OHLC, then create another set of charts of the same securities and time frames using Japanese Candlesticks along with any other analysis tool with which you are familiar or would like to observe (moving average, RSI Power Zones, etc.).

Keep in mind that for the purposes of practicing recognition of Gann's signals it is best to **plot any indicators separately on the chart (below the price bars), not overlay them on the price action.**

Lastly, I recommend keeping the colors of the charts simple, as I have done in this book. Use black OHLC bars against a white background. Some charting systems plot bars in green when the closing prices are above the opening prices, or plot in red for when the closing prices are below the opening prices. This may be helpful with your trading, but it will likely confuse you in your initial practice applying Gann's basic methods.

Gann's Writing Style and References

For those of you who have already begun your study of Gann's materials, you probably understand why I was compelled to create a subheading addressing his use of language. If you have not yet read any of Gann's materials, let me give you some examples of his style of writing to clue you into what I believe was his strategy as an author.

The Holy Bible

The first quote from the Bible that Gann presents in his writings to the public is in his first book *The Truth of the Stock Tape.* On page 51, he writes "The thing that hath been, it is that which shall be; and that which is done, is that which shall be done; and there is no new thing under the sun." (Ecclesiastes 1:9)

As you've seen in this book, Gann refers to the Bible many times. Despite your religious (or not) convictions, it may be helpful to have a copy of the Bible to refer to as such quotes are mentioned. Pay close attention to all of Gann's Bible quotes—they are very near and dear to him and he does not refer to them lightly.

Discussions of Mathematics

Gann chooses famous quotes (often Biblical) or creates his own phrases or sentences that discuss mathematics. To the casual reader they may seem sprinkled into the book, but I believe that Gann purposefully places these tenets as reminders to the greater realm within which trading and investing take place.

It's all a game of supply and demand, which can be qualified and quantified. Anything that can be quantified, therefore, is subject to the rules of the universe, which Gann clearly believes to be embedded in mathematics.

Therefore, do not glaze over these statements or quotes when you approach them in Gann's text. Instead, begin to keep track of them in a file of your own, and read through the file regularly to remind you that everything is happening in trading and investing within the context of the language of the universe—mathematics.

Whether you believe this to be true or not, you will definitely benefit from the point of view to which this keeps you attuned.

Nothing is Accidental

Gann once wrote the following: "When you make a trade, it must be on a good rule and for a good reason. There must be the possibility of a reasonable profit within a reasonable length of time.....The time limit to hold a Commodity depends upon the position you are in and the indication on your chart."

When you read sentences like these, don't be alarmed at the lack of detail. In my experience and study, very often, Gann writes such sentences mainly to bring your attention to an idea, only to explain it later on, usually through a real market example.

The best way to deal with comments like these is to not only highlight or underline them in the text, but to reiterate them in an independent outline of the key points from the chapters you are reading in any one book.

- By simply reprinting the line on another page, you acknowledge its importance.
- By reorganizing it into context with other similar tenets, you acknowledge its place.
- By reviewing it after all reading is said and done, you imprint it onto your brain—if that's not studying, I don't know what is!

Gann's use of upper-case font seems quite frequent. Take Gann's use of capitalization as an arrow pointing to information or ideas that he believes are very important for you to understand and embrace. Be sure to incorporate these elements into your outline as you study.

Gann's arrangement of rules and descriptions throughout his text is unique in that he does not always start with the most important items first. I believe that this is once again a step used to "weed out" the casual learner.

How does it work? Well, for example, when Gann presented his list of buying points in the *Commodities* book, the casual learner may have read the first couple of patterns listed, found them easy enough to understand, and then taken those rules to market application, which often ended up being a premature move.

However, the serious and dedicated learner would have read through an entire list of rules or ideas before attempting to apply any one of them, and it has been my experience with Gann's works that in this case the student is rewarded duly.

The most crucial buy rule may come in the *middle* of a list of several, properly characterized by excessive use of capitalization and all. It can then be noted and highlighted as the most crucial rule, and given top priority within the repertoire of signals ascertained from the readings.

Basically, I believe through my study experience that Gann purposefully made the most important rules and ideas ones on which serious students would focus.

I believe that even the titling of some of Gann's books is done with great purpose.

When I first came across *45 Years in Wall Street,* I had assumed this to signify that Gann spent about 45 years studying the markets. But then I came across some facts about his life. The first was that by the age of 24 he made his first trade in the commodities markets. The second was that he died at the age of 77. Clearly he had been involved with the markets for more than 50 years, so why did he create a title highlighting 45 years?

Well, referring back to the significance of eighths retracements on price, let's manipulate the eighths concept to time. We measure time in several ways, but the most straightforward method is to use calendar days. One year (Earth orbit around the Sun) is measured as approximately 365 days. During this time, the Earth moves in an elliptical orbit, 360 degrees around the sun. What is one eighth of 365 days? 45.625. And one eighth of 360 degrees? That's right, 45 degrees.

For those of you familiar with Gann's works that are using this book to revisit basic ideas, you've probably already seen the significance of the measurement "45" in trading examples or trades of your own.

For those of you who are new to Gann's works, take this example as a strong hint to pay close attention to every aspect of each work. Once again, Gann was a very deliberate writer, and being aware of that as a student will increase the value of your learning experience greatly.

Lack of Fillers

Gann generally gets right to the point of what he is trying to convey. He states the teaching as he has learned it through his study and experience, and then he provides examples to illustrate it.

At times, therefore, it may seem that reading his text is like reading an endless list of facts and tenets.

This actually can make absorption of his material more difficult for some students, as there is literally no time for the brain to rest and process if you read his text like it is a narrative.

Therefore, to help better absorb the material, especially at first when you are unfamiliar with this type of writing, take a pause (even just for a few seconds) after each page, or even paragraph. Get your mind around what you just read before moving onto the next set of ideas.

Creating Affirmations

Gann writes more than a few sentences speaking right to the reader. He creates sentences starting with "You" that describe things you should or shouldn't be doing. At first reading this, you may think it's no big deal. And some of my coaching students had a similar mindset when they started to work with me.

They'd been flooded with the rules of what NOT to do in trading that it became unclear about what TO do. That's where the mentorships that I offer make a huge difference. Because of how we build out trading plans from the ground up, and set out short-term and long-term goals.

 This was especially the case for Gerald L. He had been retired for about a year, wanted to start trading, but wanted to learn how to trade (not what to avoid) before trading the real dollars and cents in his nest egg. So that's exactly what we did. We formulated rules for Gerald to follow in his stock options trading covering all eight phases of trading. And we even created a Trading Schedule, including very specific times to check on his markets and positions for his swing trading. The rules were pivotal to help Gerald set boundaries and stay on track towards his goal.

Back to Gann's language—In order to make his statements active and useful, I took them and turned them into affirmatives. I did this with his entire list of 28 rules, and it can be applied to any other aspect of Gann's works. [Appendix B]

This skill comes with practice, and I've refined it such that I am able to take any trader's rules and guidelines and do the same.

Again, keep a running list. For example, you can convert a sentence like, "You should learn to trade on knowledge and eliminate fear and hope" (page 1 of the *Commodities* book) into "I trade on knowledge."

Eventually, you will build a list of affirmative statements that will reinforce Gann's tenets in your mind. The list will become helpful when you are in the "review" phases of trades, and even perhaps while you are managing them.

Even headings in the tables of contents in his books use "negative" language. In the *Commodities* book, just a few headings in, one reads: "Human Element the Greatest Weakness", "What to do When Commodities are Going Against You", "What to do When you Have a Series of Losses."

When you take notes on these chapters, it will help to use affirmative language to process the material. For example, under the heading "Time to Stay Out of the Market", be sure that you are focusing on what Gann is trying to convey about times to *get into* the market.

Collect Your Own Examples

Just as Gann presents trading examples in great detail with the exact days, dates, and actions in his descriptions, when you are ready to apply Gann's teachings to your charts, do the same.

From the moment you come up with a trade idea, document it on its own. If the trade entry gets filled, note that as well. As the trade plays out, document the actions you take as well as the reasons you take them, which should be part of your "Review" process anyhow.

We have the advantage in our modern world of being able to apply notes directly to our computerized charts. Your annotations don't have to be long, just clear, so that upon review of the chart or text you will know exactly what you did during that trade.

In essence, I am asking you to **track trades and examples as if you were going to write your own book delineating *your* trading methodologies**. This will likely lead to you creating a solid base of chart examples and text that add confidence to your future trading and that you can revisit and study to improve upon your skills.

A "Mentor" is an Invaluable Tool

Many of you may be learning to trade and invest in a bubble of sorts. You may not be sharing your learning adventure with your family or friends or colleagues. You may be studying when you can squeeze in the time or between other life and family commitments. I get it! So let me start by explaining how you can get started by being your OWN mentor to begin with, using 3 simple steps.:

Step 1: Where the CHARTS Have No Name

Using an image editing program (every operating system generally comes with one by default), edit out any labels on the chart which indicate the name of the security, the time axis, the price axis, or any other identifying information.

You should ultimately be left with a series of bars that are completely unlabelled. Set it aside for a while and use it in a subsequent study session when you will not remember what label had been there originally.

By doing this exercise, your inherent view of a particular market based on economics or current market conditions won't skew your analysis of the chart itself.

Step 2: Turn That CHART Upside Down

Ever hear the phrase "turn that frown upside down?" Well, now I'd like you to take a printout of that chart (or image if you need to stay digital) and *rotate it clockwise* until the original right side is now on the left and the original left side is now on the right.

Figure 8.3 and Figure 8.4 show examples of this, the first showing the original chart, and the second figure showing it in its manipulated state.

Figure 8.3

Figure 8.4

Again, since the labels are ignored, this will present an easy way to neutralize a chart by taking a downtrend and turning it into an uptrend and vice versa.

Some people are always upbeat and optimistic about the future direction of the markets and economy, and such a person is known as a permabull. On the flip side, a permabear is someone who is always down on the market with a negative view for what's ahead. But this exercise will force you to look at a market's price action in the reverse of what you just studied and analyzed. So it's great whether you're a permabull, permabear, or somewhere in the middle!

If you're permabull and tend to bring up charts with uptrends to study, this will provide you with more downtrend examples.

Please understand that this is not a reflection of how the market trades—trends don't reverse into mirror images of the preceding price action. As I discussed earlier in the book, tops and bottoms do not form in exactly the same way. However, the general sections and patterns that form in the charts will still provide useful templates with which you'll become familiar and be able to apply in future market analysis.

Step 3: Revisit the Charts

Say you intend to print out several examples for immediate study. Be sure to print two copies of the same security and time frame.

Mark up one of the two copies with what you see as you first enter into Gann's teachings. Save the chart along with its unmarked companion. Then, when you are studying at a later phase in your learning, bring those two charts back in front of you.

If you simply see additional information to mark on the studied copy, go ahead and add the new information. However if you see a set of patterns or signals which jump out at you in a new way, mark those observations on the blank copy.

Date each chart every time you mark it up. As you continue to study Gann's materials, this will help you monitor every new concept that you learn.

In my early days of learning about the markets and technical analysis, I had my father's guidance and mentorship. Having a mentor to ask my questions and help me get unstuck greatly accelerated my learning process. I also had him as a partner to review charts.

So while the self-study tactics above will help, I do strongly feel that having a mentor will greatly accelerate the process of mastering Gann's works.

That's why I started the VIP Facebook Group so that I could be accessible to you even if you are not yet one of my coaching students! You can even bounce around ideas with our Trading Tribe as a study group on our Facebook Group so that I can monitor and let you know if you are heading the wrong direction.

Be careful going off and trying to figure this out on your own. Your trading account is not simply money. It's the blood sweat and tears it took to make that money. It's your financial future and I take that seriously. It's better to study together where you have a mentor watching over you to monitor if someone has got the wrong idea and is leading you down a path that's not good for you.

I've seen it happen all too frequently and that's why I have our VIP Facebook Group as a safe space for our Trading Tribe to meet, share their wins and challenges and study together. As a student of this book, you can join us at himareddy.com/vipfb

"Go ahead, buy it, read it seriously like a student, not a trader. Underline, mark points, make notes, re-read. Don't rush for a cover to cover adventure. Give it time and effort. **This book serves as a beautiful bridge between what Mr. Gann wrote and the real life markets.**"
- Shekhar B.

I invite you to visit the HimaReddy University (himareddy.com/ gannuniversity) if you'd like to take your understanding of Gann's trading methods, and more, to the next levels.

9

Gann and Astrology

You've stayed with me through these eight chapters, covering the most important concepts focused around Gann's trading methods, and I commend you for it!

As promised, there's an entirely NEW Bonus Chapter to finish out this second edition and that is Chapter 9: Gann and Astrology. It introduces you to how astrological events may relate to trading and investing, looking at my "baby", the E-mini S&P 500 futures market, as the case study.

Basic terminology that will guide you through the chapter include:

- **The Vedas:** A collection of hymns and other ancient religious texts written in India between about 1500 and 1000 BCE
- **Vedic:** relating to the Veda or Vedas
- **Jyotish:** literally translates to "Vedic astrology and astronomy"

If this piques your interest, continue reading straight through.
If 'astrology' is outside your wheelhouse at this time remember...

Correlation does not equal causation. Keep reading with an open mind and ALWAYS use price action to confirm your entries and exits!

How Did Gann Use Astrology?

Think for a moment about the time during which Gann lived and traded. There were very strict rules, even back then, about what type of financial advice could be shared to the public or customers.

Traditional technical analysis was still looked upon very skeptically. Can you imagine how regulatory groups would have responded had Gann openly shared the specific ways he was using astrology to make some of his greatest market calls and trades? It's no wonder, then, that Gann's outward discussion of astrology is relatively small compared to his discussion of mathematical forecasting and trading methods.

However, another reason that I believe Gann whispered about astrology, as opposed to proclaiming about it loudly, is that he did not want to give the impression that it should be followed as a science. Especially not by amateurs. No matter what type of astrology you utilize, there can be no astrology without astronomy.

I'm a big fan of tennis, so I'll use that sport to explain how the two work together. Imagine a tennis court. It's got a net secured on two posts, and lines painted which delineate the service lines, base lines, and sidelines. But a tennis court doesn't come to life until players step onto it.

Let's say Rafael Nadal and Pete Sampras, my two all-time favorite players, take the court. From Nadal's perspective, he must play his tennis game not only based on the fixed elements of the court, but also in Sampras' movements and positions and speed.

Similarly, astronomy is the science upon which the foundation of the universe is laid. But to navigate one's life journey, the observation of the fixed elements of the universe relative to each other and to the moving pieces (each of us) can also be studied, though as an art.

Gann travelled the world. He spent time in India. This begs the question: did Gann use Western Astrology, or Eastern Astrology? We can never know for sure. But what I can do for you here is to help you understand the differences between these two approaches and provide sequential steps as to how to begin to use this in your trading and investing.

What is Vedic Astrology?

Terminology:

- The Vedas are a collection of hymns and other ancient religious texts written in India between about 1500 and 1000 BCE. Veda means "wisdom". This universal knowledge was imparted to the sages about 5,000 years ago when they were absorbed in a meditative state of pure consciousness.
- "Vedic" means relating to the Veda or Vedas.
- "Jyotish" literally translates to "Vedic astrology and astronomy". The word jyoti means "a flame or light". It is the light which shines down from the heavens and gives us the ability to see the physical world. It is also the light that allows us to look deeper into the subtle energies of life. The suffix -sh means "best or wisest". Therefore, the word Jyotish can be translated as the "science of light" or "the wisdom of the heavens".

I am the first person in my entire family who was born and raised in the USA, and extremely proud of it! And I also embrace my Indian heritage, with healthy doses of questioning of tradition along the way.

Growing up in a Hindu family, Jyotish has been a big part of my life. One branch of Jyotish involves selecting auspicious timing of events, to ensure the best possible outcome for those involved. It was used to pick my wedding date and time and, as well as time other key family events. I became accustomed to it as background practice, but I didn't really examine it closely.

When my father passed away in early 2016, I was reminded of the huge role that Jyotish plays in my life. Every single event or remembrance we've had for my dad was timed for the benefit of his soul as well as for the well-being of our surviving family.

So I started exploring this ancient knowledge. I began to consider Jyotish to potentially optimize the actions I choose to take in my life (personal, business, etc.). And I also use Jyotish to potentially minimize the negative effects of any astrological roadblocks or detours that may be on my path. My exploration is still in its very early phases, but it's moving along.

Given Gann's time spent in India, and my roots to the country, let's take a closer look at Vedic Astrology and break it down to understand it. I am no astrology expert, so I turn to the teachings and writings of one particular practitioner whom I have come to follow. Her name is Madhavi Rathod [17]. Madhavi's work is easy for me to understand. It has improved management of my personal and business calendars.

Prior to studying Vedic astrology, Madhavi had earned her M.B.A. and worked in the investment industry. She worked at a brokerage firm and was involved with equities and futures trading. She had her Series 7, 64, 24, and 65 securities licenses, as well as an insurance producer's license. Madhavi also worked at a mutual fund company and at a leading brokerage firm as an investment analyst in their managed money department. Thus, she can parlay her knowledge of the investment industry and the business world into her analysis of financial markets and overlay the two.

According to Madhavi, **astrology** studies the influence of the planets and stars on human life. It is the role of the astrologer to interpret the influence of these bodies on an individual's life (or a security's life). The planets continually exert a subtle energetic influence on us and on our environment. Vedic Astrology ultimately provides us with a deeper understanding of the intricate aspects of ourselves through a fuller appreciation of our destiny.

Vedic astrology is famous for its accuracy. Your natal chart is a snapshot of the placement of the planets in the heavens at the time and place of your birth. Natal charts aren't just for individuals—they can also apply to official incorporation dates for companies (stocks), or first trading dates for commodities (futures), and more.

A natal chart of an individual provides a storybook-like projection for your life from birth to death and gives insight into life purpose. We experience planetary cycles throughout our lives, which tell us about the likelihood and timing of future events. By knowing what lies ahead, you can take advantage of upcoming opportunities and minimize future obstacles.

The Hindu religion holds the tenet of *karma*. It is the principle that the sum of someone's good and bad actions in one of their lives will decide what will happen to them in their next life. Astrology can help provide deep insights into your karmic patterns and innate tendencies.

Astrology also places great emphasis on the spiritual components of an individual's life. You can use this knowledge to provide you with guidance in areas of life where you require further clarity. This, in turn, can bring more harmony and fulfillment into your life.

Western Astrology and Vedic Astrology: A Comparison

You might be wondering "Why aren't all astrology approaches considered equal, Hima? I mean we only have one sun, one moon to this earth, eight planets—or nine, depending upon how you feel about Pluto." You'd be right about those facts. The key here is that because these various elements exist, there is a choice regarding what information can be studied under any astrological discipline.

When I first started delving into financial astrology, I was also confused and conflicted as to what to use. After assessing the following, I have settled upon Vedic astrology.

According to Madhavi, here lies the simplest explanation of the differences between Western and Vedic Astrology.

Point of View

Western astrology uses the tropical zodiac, which is based on the point of view of the earth relative to the Sun and the planets. Jyotish uses the sidereal zodiac, which is based on the stars. The sidereal zodiac accounts for a phenomenon that is known as "the precession of the equinox".

To explain it most simply, the precession of the equinox ties to the axis of the Earth (upon which it rotates) being "wobbly", but in a cyclic manner. Given this wobble, the sidereal zodiac accounts for the fact that the Sun cannot return to the exact same position on the same calendar day each year; it is a few seconds of a degree off. These seconds all add up to make a degree as the years pass.

Role of the Sun

Western astrology emphasizes the Sun's relationship *to the earth and seasons*. The Vedic system is a more accurate astronomical representation of the Sun's position in relation *to the skies*.

Role of the Moon

Vedic astrology also pays more attention to your Moon sign than to your Sun sign. Jyotish incorporates the North and South nodes of the Moon—Rahu (N) and Ketu (S). The interpretation of these nodes in Vedic astrology differs from their interpretation in Western astrology.

For example, in Vedic astrology, these nodes are coequally considered as "planets" and are interpreted according to the mythology which surrounds them. As shadow planets, they have to do what is unseen and unexpected. Rahu seems to have more of a grasping nature while Ketu is forever trying to stay grounded.

Roles of the Planets

The Vedic system is a more accurate description of the placement of the planets in the heavens. In Vedic astrology, you experience planetary cycles throughout your life, which impact the occurrence of events in your life. Western astrology does not use these detailed cycles.

A note about traditional Jyotish versus modern day application includes the debate about the outer planets Neptune, Pluto, and Uranus. Five thousand years ago, these planets did not exist as per human observation from the earth.

Therefore, traditional Jyotish does not use the outer planets. However, modern Jyotish applications can include the outer planets. It's just important to realize that this won't match up with the traditional approach, if you are looking to line up the resulting analysis.

Zodiac Assignment

In Western Astrology, your ascendant (or rising sign) is determined to be in one of the 12 signs. In Jyotish, your ascendant usually shifts back one sign, or approximately 24 degrees. There are 30 degrees in any sign.

Predictive Focus

Western Astrology looks at the specifics of planetary angles (ex. Squares, trines, mid-heaven). This creates a master roadmap for observing one's life path, and adjusting plans as per the observations.

Vedic astrology utilizes various sub-charts to predict the outcome and timing of events. There are charts for your career, spouse, children, parents, health, and spiritual progress, just to name a few.

Note the following: whether you decide to proceed with Western astrology or employee Vedic analysis, the forecast created for a market will only be as precise as the information provided when determining the needle chart for the security.

This is something that always saddened my father. He was born at his parents' house in a tiny village in the state in India that is today known as Telangana. The date of his birth is an approximation; it is quite possible that it was even off by as much as a week. While he pursued the creation of natal charts around the information he had, my dad never really knew if it was based on accurate information. I, on the other hand, was born in a hospital. And the moment I came into this physical world there was a precise record taken, down to the minute, of my birth.

So how do we come up with the birth of a security? In order to best guide you, let's do a case study by walking through the market that is my "baby", the E-mini S&P 500 futures. Then, you can take this approach to any market or security that you study or trade.

Natal Chart Analysis: A Walk Through

In a pure security chart study, the study and application of cycles to your forecasting methods can provide a great guide to the likely path of future prices. Similarly, the application of astrology can provide a wonderful overview to the path of price action for a particular security. However, astrology is not a precise science.

For example, Vedic astrology typically warns that eclipses are inauspicious events, and the period of time surrounding the eclipse would not be suitable for active trading. However, this doesn't mean that every eclipse is followed by a severe market decline. On the flip side, not every auspicious date pertaining to a particular security will create a tradeable opportunity.

One of the keys to trading success is in layering unrelated analysis approaches to refine entries and exits. If you're already studying price, then add in time. If you're already studying time cycles, then consider astrology. When all three of these elements create a trading opportunity, the potential for high reward is maximized with the risk of loss minimized. That's right. I'm a big believer that **knowledge and education are the keys to being able to reduce risk while increasing reward.**

Time to dive in for our E-mini S&P 500 futures (ES) astrology case study. Here is the data I provided Madhavi regarding ES market history. Since this is a futures contract, I used the continuous chart of the ES. On TradeStation, this links the front month of each active contract to the next. This is the same way I was taught to analyze equity index futures during my Gann training courses:

The *historical low* refers to the lowest traded level on the continuous contract ES chart. This was 472.25 on Mar 6, 2009 as of the time this analysis was initiated.

During this time, the E-mini S&P 500 futures contract was in a planetary cycle and sub-cycle of 2 planets placed in the astrological house connoted to losses. It was also about a week before it changed sub-cycles. When an individual or other entity is about to make a shift in cycles, it is typically associated with an outward manifestation of this change. It can be for better or worse, depending on the significations of this change. There was also another planetary transit at this time which contributed to a downward turn.

The *historical high* refers to the highest traded level on the continuous ES chart. This was 2887.25 on Jan 29, 2018.

I provided Madhavi with the dates and prices for other key highs and lows as well: 1585.25 high on Mar 24, 2000; 694.75 low on Oct 10, 2002, and 1409.00 high on Oct 11, 2007.

After conducting her initial analysis, Madhavi followed up requesting additional information. The charts she asked for are shown, exactly as I provided them.

Figure 9.1 Chart of Jul 2007, with key highs and lows noted.
Created with ©TradeStation Technologies, Inc. All rights reserved.

High of 1401.75 on Jul 16, 2007 and low of 1290.50 on Jul 30, 2007.

Figure 9.2 Chart of Aug and Sep, 2009, with key highs and lows noted.
Created with ©TradeStation Technologies, Inc. All rights reserved.

Low of 789.75 on Aug 17, 2009 and high of 894.50 on Sep 23, 2009.

The planet Saturn made a big change in signs on Sep 9, 2009. Vedic astrology always studies Saturn carefully as it spends more time in a sign than any other planet, so it can have a greater impact than those that have more fleeting movements in the sky. Saturn moved from a planetary position that was correlated with loss and into a much stronger placement.

It takes two to three weeks to get out of the first few degrees of a new sign. It's like moving into a new house. It has to unpack and get its bearings before doing much else.

The rising sign for the E-mini S&P 500 futures chart is Virgo. The "landlord" for Virgo is the planet Mercury. Mercury is a primary indicator for commerce (which is why we pay attention to Mercury retrograde).

On Sep 23, Mercury was at home in Virgo, which made it very strong, and it was retrograde (also seen as a sign of strength as it is closer to earth and more impactful). Plus, Mercury also had gained what we would translate as "planetary dignity" in the chart. So it was three times stronger than usual.

Mercury is important in this instance due to the fact that the ES chart was in a major Mercury cycle. It was in a sub-cycle of Jupiter. On Sep 23, Jupiter was also retrograde (hence adding more power), plus it was back in its natal position (i.e. where it was "at birth"). From this position, it was able to astrologically "influence" Mercury.

Figure 9.3 Chart of Jul and Aug, 2012 with key highs and lows noted.
Created with ©TradeStation Technologies, Inc. All rights reserved.

Low of 1196.00 on Jul 12, 2012 and high of 1301.00 on Aug 21, 2012.

Figure 9.4 Chart of Jan, Feb, and Mar, 2014 with key highs and lows noted.
Created with ©TradeStation Technologies, Inc. All rights reserved.

High of 1758.75 on Jan 15, 2014. Low of 1645.25 on Feb 3, 2014. High of 1800.50 on Mar 7, 2014.

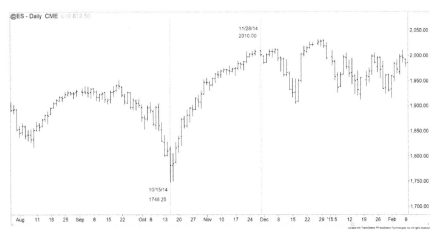

Figure 9.5 Chart of Oct and Nov 2014 with highs and lows noted.
Created with ©TradeStation Technologies, Inc. All rights reserved.

Low of 1748.25 on Oct 15, 2014 and high of 2010.00 on Nov 28, 2014.

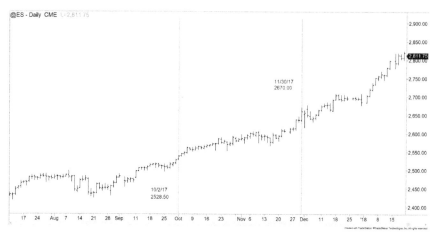

Figure 9.6 Chart of Oct and Nov 2017 with highs and lows for the months.
Created with ©TradeStation Technologies, Inc. All rights reserved.

Low of 2528.50 on Oct 2, 2017 and high of 2670.00 on Nov 30, 2017.

Upon providing this information, Madhavi began detailed analysis. Now, we'll walk through some of her findings and observations as they relate to ES price history and astrology.

Saturn moved out of Scorpio at the end of October 2017 and entered Sagittarius. Saturn was moving from Scorpio (which is classified as "a water sign") to Sagittarius (which is classified as "a fire sign"). Whenever Saturn moves from one sign to another, it portends a lot of ups and downs, akin to what happens to us when we move residences. Moveover, when Saturn moves from a water sign to a fire sign, it is the most unstable as the elements are so disparate, i.e. water puts out fire. A planet is not considered stable in a new sign till it passes the first 3 degrees of the sign. Thus, it no longer has just "one foot in the door". Saturn passed the 3 degree mark at the end of Nov.

Saturn's entry into Sagittarius also gave the S&P 500 futures market some breathing room. In the birth chart for the S&P 500 futures market, the Moon is placed in Scorpio. As you may recall, Vedic astrology is a lunar-based system and relies heavily on the Moon.

When the Moon and Saturn are together, the Moon often feels constricted by Saturn. This is more so if there are no other planets (i.e. Jupiter) to offset Saturn's heavy gaze. Saturn is typically thought of as being restrictive. They also are contrasting energetically. Saturn moves every 2.5- 3 years. The Moon moves every 2.5 days. It's hard for them to keep pace with each other. Even though the Moon moves every 2.5 days, its natal or birth placement does not change, and that takes precedence over anything else. When Saturn comes to visit by transit every 28 years or so, the Moon feels some loss of its luminosity.

Figure 9.7, E-mini S&P 500 futures, continuous contract, daily
Created with ©TradeStation Technologies, Inc. All rights reserved.

On Jan 31, 2018, a total eclipse was visible in the United States. The ES futures markets trades on the Chicago Mercantile Exchange (CME) headquartered in Chicago, IL.

As per Vedic astrology, eclipses are considered inauspicious. This is because the luminaries (the Sun and the Moon) are occluded. So during eclipses, humans can not see in the right (normal) light.

We may not always have complete information when making a trade or may act on information which we believe to be accurate, but may not be. In trading, we can be subject to seeing only one side of the evidence, or being influenced by one-time events that override our analysis of the trends and patterns.

Therefore, during eclipses traders may run into factors which they don't see or are unaware of, which can lead to making improper judgments. Therefore, as per Vedic astrology, eclipses are a poor time for trading and generally lead to falling prices.

A major high formed on Jan 29, 2018, just ahead of the eclipse date. Then, on Feb 1, 2018, the Moon was in a constellation which had been previously eclipsed. Eclipses tend to be problematic. They can have a negative impact on the market. These back to back events set the stage for unfavorable activity. Vedic astrology is a multifaceted subject. We look at the twelve astrological signs in the zodiac, the nine planets, the birth chart, and planetary movements or transits.

Just as we may overlay multiple trend charts on top of each other to render an analysis, an astrologer must consider a multiple of factors to determine what impact an event will have on a person or entity. An additional consideration in Vedic astrology is the lunar constellation that the Moon occupies on a given day. Each has its own nuances. On Feb 6, the Moon was in a constellation which symbolizes great instability. As the trading chart shows, the S&P 500 future market had wide market fluctuations that day.

The subsequent price action shows a severe decline of prices into Feb 6, 2018, posting a low at 2537.75.

Therefore, if a trader had an astrological roadmap of the ES coming into late Jan 2018, he may have been better prepared for this sudden downturn in prices.

Figure 9.8, E-mini S&P 500 futures, continuous contract, daily.
Created with ©TradeStation Technologies, Inc. All rights reserved.

Toward the end of October 2017, Jupiter changed zodiacal signs. Jupiter changes signs about once a year. Jupiter moved in mid October from Libra to Scorpio. By virtue of doing so, Jupiter joined the Moon in the S&P Futures chart. When Jupiter and Moon combine in a Vedic astrology chart, it's a combination for mutual collaboration amongst entities. It enhances both parties. The Moon also represents the masses or the public. Jupiter represents (good) fortune. In astrology, each sign has a "landlord". Since Vedic astrology does not use the outer planets, they differ somewhat between Vedic and Western. When Jupiter made its foray into Scorpio, it was moving into a more friendly habitat. It took about two weeks for Jupiter to stabilize in its new home.

Once it did so at the end of October 2018, then the S&P 500 reflected this accordingly. In this chart, you can see that the ES market stabilized on Oct 29, 2018 posting a low at 2612.50, then rallied accordingly.

Additionally, the S&P 500 futures chart was in a sub-cycle of Jupiter when it moved, so that provided greater support.

Figure 9.9, E-mini S&P 500 futures, continuous contract, daily
Created with ©TradeStation Technologies, Inc. All rights reserved.

On Nov 2, 2014, Saturn changed signs. Saturn entered Libra, which is its sign of greatest strength. This was a stabilizing move, and was reinforced by the roughly two weeks of prior strong market action. Saturn moves slowly but can create a long-lasting impact. By moving into Libra, Saturn was positioned to provide long-term greater gains. They were not immediately evident, but you can see that the long term trend from Nov, 2014 to October, 2017 was up.

Bringing Astrology Into Your Trading Business

If you're a specialist, only trading 1-5 markets, which I highly recommend, then getting the natal chart work done for those markets will turbo charge your understanding of that market's behavior, especially its cycles. And that's actually why I introduced this chapter on Gann and astrology in this second edition, because it is something that I have learned makes a huge difference, so much so that I always recommend it to my coaching students.

It bears repeating. I HIGHLY recommend focusing on just 1-5 securities to day trade or swing trade. That's one of the first aspects of fine tuning your Trading Plan that we work on in coaching.

Not only does it help you keep your trading consistent, you are also primed to incorporate financial astrology into your trading business.

If you are currently a generalist, trading all types of markets as long as they fit your parameters for a setup, you can still benefit from financial astrology guidance by applying it to the broad market that guides your picks. The S&P 500 is "the" market to follow, but you could also look to the Dow, Nasdaq, or Russell, again depending upon your underlying assets that you trade.

 For example, one coaching student, Shelly P., trades the SPY very closely and has developed a trading plan that includes just a few other stocks for options trading as well. Shelly's in the best position to bring financial astrology into her trading because she'll only need to focus on the leading planets and natal charts for a handful of markets.

"Thank you so much for all your education and training over the last few months of mentoring. This is a lifelong process of learning and continued growth and I appreciate the opportunity to learn from you. ~ Shelly P., California

The End...of the Beginning

Congratulations! You've completed this first primer into Gann's work!

Did you know that over 90% of people never read beyond Chapter 2 in ANY book? That you have continued the journey this far means that you are seriously vested in your trading education, and I commend you!

I hope you can see that many of Gann's trading methods are straightforward enough to apply to your current market study. There are several Gann tools that we've explored in this book and can consider in *any* market environment.

The Gann patterns may work best for you when applied within the context of your existing trading "tool box"—whether that includes oscillators, studies on the price chart, candlesticks, Fibonacci, etc., confluence is the key. Gann's methods are simple enough to add to other analysis tools already in play, as suggested by the subtitle of this book.

Learning the buying and selling patterns will probably be a bit like learning to ride a bicycle. You will need to practice and get a hang of recognizing the signals. I recommended following them "on paper" before applying them to your live account. That's sort of like your training wheels.

Then, as you build confidence in your ability to recognize the patterns and plan sound trades around them (remember CAPITAL PRESERVATION), the training wheels can come off and you can slowly incorporate these tools into your trading plan.

My goal in writing this book was to provide students like you a guide to mastering Gann's works. I wanted to write THE book that didn't exist when I was 16 years old and first handed the *Commodities* book by my dad, or just never did find. I hope that you have found value in what I've presented and that I've inspired you to take the next step towards trading success!

As I mentioned throughout this book, in writing this second edition I surveyed my traders and asked for their advice on what they likely to include.

One trader wrote in, saying, "I would request you keep the content from the first edition and add to it the wisdom you have gained since it was published."

That is what I strived to do and I hope that your experience in reading this book also ignites a love for the lifelong study of Gann.

Talk Soon!
Hima

P.S. And for any bits of wisdom that didn't come through along the way, remember, there's nothing like learning from your mentor in an interactive way.

I invite you to visit the HimaReddy University (himareddy.com/gannuniversity) if you'd like to take your understanding of Gann's trading methods, and more, to the next levels.

[17] If you are interested in having your own Vedic Charts, I highly recommend Madhavi Rathod at vedichealing.com. Madhavi's experience with Vedic astrology, as well as being a trader herself, has made her insights invaluable to my trading business and I recommend her services to all of my coaching students.

APPENDIX A

Gann's 28 Trading Rules

This is the original list from the book *How to Make Profits Trading in Commodities* with slight edits to account for additional wording used in the *45 Years on Wall Street* book.

#1: Amount of capital to use: Divide your capital into 10 equal parts and never risk more than one-tenth of your capital on any one trade.

#2: Use stop loss orders. Always protect a trade when you make it with a stop loss order 1 to 3 cents, never more than 5 cents away, cotton 20 to 40, never more than 60 points away. (3 to 5 points away for stocks)

#3: Never overtrade. This would be violating your capital rules.

#4: Never let a profit run into a loss. After you once have a profit of 3 cents or more, raise your stop loss order so that you will have no loss of capital. For cotton when the profits are 60 points or more place stop where there will be no loss.

#5: Do not buck the trend. Never buy or sell if you are not sure of the trend according to your charts and rules.

#6: When in doubt, get out, and don't get in when in doubt.

#7: Trade only in active markets. Keep out of slow, dead ones.

#8: Equal distribution of risk. Trade in 2 or 3 different commodities, if possible. (Trade in 4 or 5 stocks, is possible.) Avoid tying up all your capital in any one commodity.

#9: Never limit your orders or fix a buying or selling price. Trade at the market.

#10: Don't close your trades without a good reason. Follow up with a stop loss order to protect your profits.

#11: Accumulate a surplus. After you have made a series of successful trades, put some money into a surplus account to be used only in emergency or in times of panic.

#12: Never buy or sell just to get a scalping profit.

#13: Never average a loss. This is one of the worst mistakes a trader can make.

#14: Never get out of the market just because you have lost patience or get into the market because you are anxious from waiting.

#15: Avoid taking small profits and big losses.

#16: Never cancel a stop loss order after you have placed it at the time you make a trade.

#17: Avoid getting in and out of the market too often.

#18: Be just as willing to sell short as you are to buy. Let your object be to keep with the trend and make money.

#19: Never buy just because the price of a commodity is low or sell short just because the price is high

#20: Be careful about pyramiding at the wrong time. Wait until the commodity is very active and has crossed Resistance Levels before buying more and until it has broken out of the zone of distribution before selling more.

#21: Select the commodities that show strong uptrend to pyramid on the buying side and the ones that show definite downtrend to sell short.

#22: Never hedge. If you are long of one commodity and it starts to go down, do not sell another commodity short to hedge it. Get out at the market; take your loss and wait for another opportunity.

#23: Never change your position in the market without good reason. When you make a trade, let it be for some good reason or according to some definite rule; then do not get out without a definite indication of a change in trend.

#24: Avoid increasing your trading after a long period of success or a period of profitable trades.

#25: Don't' guess when the market is top. Let the market prove it is top. Don't guess when the market is bottom. Let the market prove it is bottom. By following definite rules, you can do this.

#26: Do not follow another man's advice unless you know that he knows more than you do.

#27: Reduce trading after the first loss; never increase.

#28: Avoid getting in wrong and out wrong; getting in right and out wrong; this is making double mistakes.

APPENDIX B

Affirmative Versions of Gann's 28 Rules

Gann Rule (Affirmative) #1: Divide your capital into 10 equal parts and always risk less than one-tenth of your capital on any one trade.

Gann Rule (Affirmative) #2: Use stop loss orders. Always protect a trade when you make it with a stop loss order (on commodities) 1 to 3 cents (up to 5 cents) away. For cotton, 20 to 40 points (up to 60 points) away. For stocks, 3 to 5 points away.

Gann Rule (Affirmative) #3: Always trade lot sizes and amounts of risk that fit within the limits of your capital.

Gann Rule (Affirmative) #4: Always protect your accumulated profit. On a long position, raise your stop loss order once your profit equals your initial risk. On a short position, lower your stop loss order once your profit equals your initial risk.

Gann Rule (Affirmative) #5: Trade with the trend. Only buy or sell if you are sure of the trend according to your chart and rules.

Gann Rule (Affirmative) #6: Only enter the market and stay in a trade so long as you are sure of the market indications according to your rules.

Gann Rule (Affirmative) #7: Trade only in active markets.

Gann Rule (Affirmative) #8: Distribute risk equally among traded markets. Only risk up to 10 percent of your capital in any one market.

Gann Rule (Affirmative) #9: Let the market show you at what price to enter a buy or a sell.

Gann Rule (Affirmative) #10: Only close your trade with a good reason. Follow up with a stop loss order to protect your profits.

Gann Rule (Affirmative) #11: Accumulate a surplus. After you have made a series of successful trades, put some money into a surplus account as an emergency fund.

Gann Rule (Affirmative) #12: Trade the swings in accordance with the existing trend. This is where you can make the most profit for the least number of trades.

Gann Rule (Affirmative) #13: Only pyramid on trades that are showing profit. This is how you can make the most profits on sustained moves.

Gann Rule (Affirmative) #14: Only enter and exit the market on definite signals with emotions in check.

Gann Rule (Affirmative) #15: Take large profits and small losses.

Gann Rule (Affirmative) #16: Once you've placed a stop loss order, always keep it, and only move it in the direction which minimizes risk/protects profits.

Gann Rule (Affirmative) #17: Trade only when you have definite signals.

Gann Rule (Affirmative) #18: Be just as willing to sell short as you are to buy. Let your object be to keep with the trend and make money.

Gann Rule (Affirmative) #19: Buy only when you have definite indication of a rising market. Sell only when you have definite indication of a falling market.

Gann Rule (Affirmative) #20: Pyramid at the right time. On a long position, wait until the security is very active and has crossed Resistance Levels before buying more. On a short position, wait until the security has broken out of the zone of distribution before selling more.

Gann Rule (Affirmative) #21: Select the commodities that show strong uptrend to pyramid on the buying side and the ones that show definite downtrend to sell short.

Gann Rule (Affirmative) #22: If you have a position on and the market starts to move against it, get out at the market, take your loss, and wait for another opportunity. Or, rely on your stop order to minimize your losses.

Gann Rule (Affirmative) #23: Only change your position in the market with a good reason. When you make a trade, let it be for some good reason or according to some definite rule; then stay in the trade until you have a definite indication of a change in trend.

Gann Rule (Affirmative) #24: Maintain your lot size and maximum risk amount after a long period of success or a period of profitable trades. (Only increase your lot size and maximum risk amount after you have doubled your capital and added back half to your initial account size, increasing your total tradable capital amount).

Gann Rule (Affirmative) #25: Let the market prove it is making a top. Let the market prove it is making a bottom. By following definite rules, you can do this.

Gann Rule (Affirmative) #26: Only follow another man's advice if you know that he knows more than you do.

Gann Rule (Affirmative) #27: If your lot size contains multiple contracts, reduce the number of contracts traded after the first loss.

Gann Rule (Affirmative) #28: Focus on getting in the market according to your rules and out of the market according to your rules.

APPENDIX C

GANN BUYING POINTS

Gann Buying Point #1: "BUY at OLD BOTTOMS or OLD TOP...Buy when..any commodity..declines 1c to 3 c under old tops or bottoms."

Gann Buying Point #2: SAFER BUYING POINT. Buy when wheat, cotton or any commodity crosses a series of tops of previous weeks, showing that the minor or the main trend has turned up as indicated by the charts on individual commodities.

Gann Buying Point #3: "SAFEST BUYING POINT. Buy on a secondary reaction after wheat, cotton or any commodity has crossed previous weekly tops and the advance exceeds the greatest rally on the way down from the top."

Gann Buying Point #4: "BUY when the first rally from the extreme bottom exceeds in time the greatest rally in the preceding Bear Campaign"

Gann Buying Point #5: "BUY when the period of time exceeds the last rally before extreme lows were reached. If the last rally was 3 or 4 weeks, when the advance from the bottom is more than 3 or 4 weeks, consider the trend has turned up and commodities are a safer buy on a secondary reaction."

Gann Buying Point #6: BUY AFTER BREAKAWAY POINTS ARE CROSSED ON INDIVIDUAL COMMODITIES. The market will then be in the runaway move where you can make large profits in a short period of time.

Gann Buying Point #7: BUY when wheat, corn, cotton or any commodity declines to 50% of highest selling prices, or to ½ or 50% range between extreme high or extreme low prices. This is one of the safe buying points as we will prove later by examples of past market movements. When there is a 50% reaction of the last move up, it becomes a buying point so long as the main trend is up……

Gann Buying Point #8: "BUY against double or triple bottoms, or buy on first, second or third higher bottom and buy a second lot after wheat, soy beans or cotton makes second or third higher bottom, then crosses previous top."

Gann Buying Point #9: "BUYING RULES FOR RAPID ADVANCES AT HIGH LEVELS. In the last stages of a Bull Market in a commodity, reactions are small. Buy on 2-day reactions and follow up with STOP LOSS ORDER 1c to 2c under each day's low level. Then when the low of a previous day is broken you will be out. Markets sometimes run 10 to 30 days without breaking low of previous day."

GANN SELLING POINTS

Gann Selling Point #1: "SELL at OLD TOPS or OLD BOTTOMS…"

Gann Selling Point #2: SAFER SELLING POINT. Sell when wheat, soy beans, cotton, or any commodity breaks the low of a previous week or a series of bottoms of previous weeks as indicated by the trend and rules.

Gann Selling Point #3: "SAFEST SELLING POINT. Sell on a *secondary rally* after wheat, soy beans, cotton or any commodity has broken the previous bottoms of several weeks or has broken the bottom of the last reaction, turning trend down. This secondary rally nearly always comes after the first sharp decline in the first section of Bear Campaign."

Gann Selling Point #4: "SELL after the first decline exceeds the greatest reaction in the preceding Bull Campaign or the last reaction before final top."

Gann Selling Point #5: "Sell after BREAKAWAY POINT is crossed."

Gann Selling Point #6: "Sell when the period of time of the first decline exceeds the last reaction before final top of the Bull Campaign. Example: If wheat or any commodity has advanced for several months of for one year of more, and the greatest reaction has been four weeks, which is an average reaction in a Bull Market, then after top is reached and the first decline runs more than 4 weeks, it is an indication of a change in the minor trend or the main trend. The commodity will be a safer short sale on any rally because you will be trading with the trend after it has been definitely defined."

Gann Selling Point #7: SELL at 50% or ½ oint of last high to low of sharp decline or sell at 50% of highest selling point or 50% of greatest range. Sell when wheat, soy beans, cotton, or any commodity rallies 50% of a previous move down…"

Gann Selling Point #8: "SELL against Double Tops or Triple Tops, or SELL when the market makes lower tops or lower bottoms. It is safe to sell when wheat, soy beans, or cotton, makes a second, third, or fourth, lower top, also safe to sell after *double* and *triple bottoms* are broken. "

Gann Selling Point #9: "SELL in the last stages of Bear Market or when there is rapid decline and only 2 days rallies and follow down with stop loss order 1 cent above the high of the previous day. When wheat or any commodity rallies 1 cent or more above the high of the previous day you will be out on *stop*. Fast declining markets will often run 10 to 30 days without crossing high of the previous day."

APPENDIX D

Gann's Soybean Chart

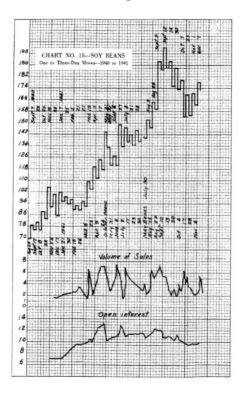

**Download and Print your Companion Guide
with full size and full color charts and get your
Video Walkthroughs at
himareddy.com/gann2bonus**

APPENDIX E

Google, Inc. (GOOG) Highs and Lows
by Calendar Month

Jan

F - $475.11 high (Jan 11, 2006)

P - $629.51 high (Jan 4, 2010)

R - $642.92 high (Jan 19, 2011)

V - $670.25 high (Jan 4, 2012)

Feb

B - $216.80 high (Feb 2, 2005)

Mar

C - $172.57 low (Mar 14, 2005)

G - $331.55 low (Mar 10, 2006)

I - $437.00 low (Mar 5, 2007)

M - $412.11 low (Mar 17, 2008)

N - $602.45 high (Mar 2, 2008)

Apr

May

Jun

S - $473.02 low (Jun 24, 2011)

Jul

D - $317.80 high (Jul 21, 2005)

J - $558.58 high (Jul 16, 2007)

Q - $433.63 low (Jul 1, 2010)

T - $627.50 high (Jul 26, 2011)

Aug

A - $95.96 extreme low (Aug 19, 2004)

E - $273.35 low (Aug 22, 2005)

K - $480.46 low (Aug 16, 2007)

September

Oct

U - $480.60 low (Oct 4, 2011)

Nov

L - $747.24 extreme high (Nov 7, 2007)

H - $513.00 high (Nov 22, 2006)

O - $247.30 low (Nov 21, 2008)

December

I invite you to visit the HimaReddy University (himareddy.com/gannuniversity) if you'd like to take your understanding of Gann's trading methods to the next levels.

Hima Reddy, at only 16 years old, started learning futures from her dad, a successful trader in the Gann style of trading.

She studied finance at Indiana University's Kelly School of Business, and then immersed herself in study of the markets upon her return to New York in 2001.

Hima became very involved with the Chartered Market Technicians Association, helping develop their exams as well as member events and conferences. She also interfaced with universities across the country, bringing technical analysis to upcoming finance students. All the while trading equity and commodity futures while completing her certification. She worked as a Senior Technical Analyst at Piper Jaffray (now Piper Sandler) before going it on her own to help traders directly.

Hima's 'mentor' has always been Gann and to this day his book, *How to Make Profits Trading in Commodities* is her go-to guide to the markets. She particularly focuses her analysis on Gann pattern recognition and time duration relationships.

Over the past 20+ years, she has helped hundreds of thousands of individuals create a sound plan for their financial future, appearing in the WallStreet Journal, Barrons, Bloomberg, Reuters, TheStreet, NBC, CNBC, Fox, ABC, and more. Her passion has always been carrying on her father's legacy by helping dedicated traders achieve their financial freedom.

You can find out more and get free, instant access to Hima's Hot, Timely and Actionable market picks and tips at himareddy.com

CPSIA information can be obtained
at www.ICGtesting.com
Printed in the USA
LVHW081029040323
740549LV00002B/23